Charles D'Ambrosio's essay collection *Orphans* spawned something of a cult following. In the decade since the tiny limited-edition volume sold out its print run, its devotees have pressed it upon their friends, students, and colleagues, only to find themselves begging for their copy's safe return. For anyone familiar with D'Ambrosio's writing, this enthusiasm should come as no surprise. His work is exacting and emotionally generous, often as funny as it is devastating. *Loitering* gathers those eleven original essays with new and previously uncollected work, so that a broader audience might discover one of our great living essayists. No matter his subject—Native American whaling, a Pentecostal "hell house," Mary Kay Letourneau, the work of J. D. Salinger, or, most often, his own family—D'Ambrosio approaches each piece with a singular voice and searching point of view; each essay, while unique and surprising, is unmistakably his own.

PRAISE FOR
LOITERING

"We can see he is one of the strongest, smartest and most literate essayists practicing today. This, one would hope, is his moment. . . . These [essays] are highly polished, finished, exemplary performances."

—PHILLIP LOPATE, *New York Times Book Review* (An Editors' Choice)

"*Loitering*, by Charles D'Ambrosio, gets something deeply right about being uncertain, being in-between, being human. Its essays refuse the violence of imposing too much resolution on the world. This praise might sound abstract, but it's more like a kind of closed-eye, clenched-fist gratitude: Thank you. These essays help me believe in what's holy in the mess."

—LESLIE JAMISON, *New York Times*

"Maybe it's odd to call a book kind, but kindness seems to be *Loitering*'s animating principle. 'Alone,' D'Ambrosio writes . . . 'you're vastly outnumbered; but in the company of another, by some weird miracle of human math, the odds seem wonderfully improved in your favor.' That is it, the essence of why this book is so very good: it delivers that most primal pleasure of reading—the feeling of being understood, of not being alone."

—ANNALISA QUINN, NPR Books

"D'Ambrosio hasn't published anything less than brilliant, but *Loitering* is remarkable even by his standards."

—MICHAEL SCHAUB, *Portland Mercury*

"Important . . . one of the most profound essayists at work today."

—J. C. HALLMAN, *Bookforum*

"As a witness to human longing and delusion, D'Ambrosio is among our most eloquent voices. Reading *Loitering* I thought about David Foster Wallace a lot. D'Ambrosio is a different sort of writer: more personal, more openly haunted, preoccupied by the rites of Catholicism. But he shares with Foster Wallace a gift for exactitude, erudition, and moral concern. Both take an obvious delight in language as an instrument of truth—and perhaps more so as a weapon in the war against the American habit of falsehood."

—STEVE ALMOND, *The Daily Beast*

"What I admired most about these essays is the way each one takes its own shape, never conforming to an expected narrative or feeling the need to answer all the questions housed within. D'Ambrosio allows his essays their ambivalence, and this gives ideas space to move freely across time."

—HANNAH GERSEN, *The Millions*

"Powerful . . . highlights D'Ambrosio's ability to mine his personal history for painful truths about the frailty of family and the strange quest to understand oneself, and in turn, be understood. "

—*Publishers Weekly*, Starred Review

"In every essay, D'Ambrosio keenly displays one vital skill a nonfiction writer can't fake: observation. . . . He transforms everyday experiences, uncertainty and all, into perfect stories."

—TIFFANY GIBERT, *Time Out New York*

"*Loitering: New & Collected Essays* should help position D'Ambrosio as one of the major essayists now working in the genre."

—ADAM FLEMING PETTY, *Los Angeles Review of Books*

LOITERING

LOITERING

NEW &
COLLECTED
ESSAYS

**CHARLES
D'AMBROSIO**

 TIN HOUSE BOOKS / Portland, Oregon & Brooklyn, New York

Published by Tin House Books, Portland, Oregon and Brooklyn, New York

Distributed to the trade by Publishers Group West, 1700 Fourth St., Berkeley, CA 94710, www.pgw.com

Library of Congress Cataloging-in-Publication Data

D'Ambrosio, Charles.
  [Essays. Selections]
  Loitering : new & collected essays / Charles D'Ambrosio.
    pages cm
  ISBN 978-1-935639-87-9 (paperback)
  I. Title.
  PS3554.A469A6 2014
  814.54—dc22
  2014014455

First U.S. Edition 2014
Third Printing 2016
Printed in the USA
Interior design by Jakob Vala

www.tinhouse.com

For all the conversations over the years this book goes out to Drew Bouton, Jon Fontana, and Tom Grimes; and I also send it along with love to some dear people who talked me up, talked me down, and talked me through, Marilyn Davis, Jae Choi, and my sisters; and of course the soul of the book belongs to Mike and Danny, my brothers, who will never read a word of it, though their silence tunes every sentence I write.

CONTENTS

By Way of a Preface........................ 13

PART 1: WEST OF THE WEST

Seattle, 1974 27
Loitering 41
Whaling Out West 63
Catching Out 91
This Is Living 97
Documents 121

PART 2: STRATEGIES AGAINST EXTINCTION

American Newness 135
Winning 147
Hell House 163
One More Paradise 179
Orphans 197

PART 3: READING LIFE

Salinger and Sobs 227
Misreading 263
Casting Stones 273
Doo-Wop Down the Road 299
Any Resemblance to Anyone Living 309
Degrees of Gray in Philipsburg 320

By Way of a Preface

There's an old bus stop in Seattle that's maybe the lone-
liest place in the world for me, and it was there, reading
in the vague light, that I first discovered the essay. Even
now when I drive by, I still check that stop, looking for
one of my brothers or sisters, although the stop itself
has been moved to a better location and the family I
might give a lift to is gone. By the standards of the day
it was an excellent place to wait for the bus, really the
stoop of an apartment, with a marble stairway that was
cold but covered, offering shelter from the wind and
the rain and a lighted entry that was just bright enough
to read by. You had to sit on the top step and slouch
over and futz with the book to get the angle, but once
you had it, the words resolved on the page. As a bonus

there was a bookstore across the street that stayed open late. It was one of those small places that made up for a lack of inventory with sensibility, a bookstore you could trust, and the first that I knew of to hand out free book-marks, which I thought at the time was infinitely clever. I had just figured out, rather naïvely, that I could buy my own books, and then almost instantly I became a prig about their condition, so much so that I wouldn't lend them to anyone, at least not without a solemn lecture about their proper handling: no breaking the spines, no dog-earing the pages, no greasy thumbprints. At home, I had my own somewhat wobbly arrange-ment of brick-and-board shelves, two and then three tiers of ugly pressboard, painted brown and laddered up against the wall, my first piece of furniture. In pri-vate, I thought of those shelves with enormous pride, as something I was building, book by book, and brick by brick, and I often looked at them, vaguely satisfied, like a worker inspecting the progress of a job. I wanted the shelves to rise up and reach the ceiling, and for that to happen, all I had to do, I realized, was read.

My sense of the essay as a genre isn't something I can separate from my experience of those early encoun-ters. I bought my first collection from that little book-store, on their recommendation, and fell in love with the writer M. F. K. Fisher, whose works on gastronomy couldn't have been more foreign to me, growing up, as I did, in a big family, where we boiled everything in vats, drank powdered milk, and my father, fielding a complaint about food, would clench the fist of his free hand and stab his fork at the offending item on his plate and say, "Eat it. Your stomach doesn't care." Well into adulthood I was too shy to pepper food at a restaurant, afraid that I would somehow be insulting the cook. Anyway, it was at family meals that we learned indifference to our bodies, but it was in prose, particularly the kind I found in the personal essay, that a relationship to that body began to be restored, at least for me. One of my earliest ideas about writing was that the rhythms of prose came from the body, and although I still believe that, I still don't know what I mean. I would discover, eventually, that some of Fisher's love of food was a celebratory rebellion against a similar tyranny at home, a rejection of the dulling rules and sumptuary restrictions of the dinner table set by her grandmother. Prose moves so mysteriously that I believe I heard this unstated fact in the rhythm of her sentences long before her biography confirmed it. It came to me sotto voce, whispered on a lower frequency, a secret shared between intimates. And so, while the superficial subject of Fisher's essays may have drawn me in, offering a fantasy world in which foie gras and Dom Pérignon mattered, soon enough it was language itself, and more specifically, the right she assumed to be exact about her life, that won me completely. More than the wonders of Provence or advice on how to serve peacock tongues on toast, it was her prose that taught me how to pay attention, and it was the essay, as a form, that was the container, the thing that caught and held the words like holy water, offering the gift of awareness, the simple courtesy of acknowledgment, even to a life as ordinary as mine.

Other essayists followed, and I read them in great passionate jags—all of Joan Didion and George Orwell, all of Susan Sontag and Samuel Johnson, all of Edward Abbey and Hunter Thompson and James Baldwin, living for weeks at a time within the sentences of a single writer, excluding other authors, other kinds of reading. I read poems and novels promiscuously but essays were my fast friends. Something in the nature of the personal essay must have instructed me and informed this pattern. And I must have needed that sort of close attachment, that guidance, the voice holding steady in the face of doubt, the flawed man revealing his flaws, the outspoken woman simply *saying*, the brother and the sister—for essays were never a father to me, nor a mother. Essays were the work of equals, confiding, uncertain, solitary, free, and even the best of them had an unfinished feel, a tentative note, that made them approachable. A good essay seemed to question itself in a way that a novel or short story did not—or perhaps it was simply that the personal essay left its questions on the page, there for everyone to see; it was a forum for self-doubt, for an attempt whose outcome wasn't assured. That one mind would speak so candidly to another mind held a special appeal to me at a time when I didn't even know I had such a thing. Late at night, sitting on a cold stoop, waiting for the bus, the free and easy conversations I fell into via the essay seemed to suit my station in life perfectly.

For a glimpse inside the essence of the essay as I felt it then, as I understand it now, I'd like to misuse this passage from Patricia Hampl.

> On the first page of the *Confessions* [Augustine] poses a problem that has a familiar modern ring: "... it would seem clear that no one can call upon Thee without knowing Thee." There is, in other words, the problem of God's notorious absence. Augustine takes the next step West; he seeks his faith *with* his doubt: "... may it be that a man must implore Thee before he can know Thee?" The assumption here is that faith is not to be confused with certainty; the only thing people can really count on is longing and the occult

directives of desire. So, Augustine wonders, does that mean prayer must come *before* faith? Illogical as it is, perhaps not-knowing is the first condition of prayer, rather than its negation. Can that be?

Seeking faith with doubt, that's definition enough for me. Or strike faith, if you must, and leave it at seeking with doubt. And longing. And not-knowing. And the occult directives of desire.

And taking the next step West.

I wrote the earliest of these essays for *The Stranger* in Seattle because no one else would give me five thousand words and then agree not to change a single comma—exactly the kind of hard bargain you can strike when you're willing to work for next to nothing. While the pay wasn't fancy, the freedom was absolute, and at that time in my life the liberty to think and write as I pleased mattered far more than money. I will always feel deeply indebted to *The Stranger*, and nothing satisfies me more than to acknowledge those foolhardy souls in this preface.

I worked on each of these pieces a stupidly long time, with a determination that was fueled, in part, by vanity. I wanted the writing to live an independent life and not rely on passing opinion or the ephemeral realities of alt-weeklies and magazines to make its way in the world. Rather insufferably I thought of myself as an essayist and bristled when friends and family, in conversation, referred to my published work as "articles." The subjects of these pieces mattered, of course, but it was important to me that the sentences alone do the convincing. What this meant in actual practice was that I often had no idea what I was doing, no plan or sense of purpose, until I started putting words on paper. I relied on my ear to a ridiculous extent, trusting that if I got the sound right— the music, the mood, the feel of things—then sense might eventually make an appearance. Sometimes sense showed up, and other times, in that tussle of trial and error at the heart of all writing, error won the day. My instinctive and entirely private ambition was to capture the conflicted mind in motion, or, to borrow a phrase from Cioran, to represent failure on the move, so leaving a certain wrongness on the page was OK by me. The inevitable errors and imperfections made the trouble I encountered tactile, bringing the texture of experience into the story in a way that being cautiously right never could. In fact, as much as I wrote and rewrote many of these pieces, often, in a contrary mood, the goal of those revisions was to get the thing to read like a rough draft, cutting sonorities of thought and style that seemed dishonest, fighting against the insane clarity of public discourse or, in the more personal pieces, scraping away until I renewed my sympathies for raw subjects that time and habit had turned sclerotic.

Many of the ideas were mine, but just as often the impetus for these essays came to me in the form of assignments, which was always a rush, like being dropped behind enemy lines with nothing but a brick and a can of beans and the essayist's motto: *Que sais-je?* Very often I knew nothing. That's when the subject got its revenge, obligating me in ethical ways to justify my arbitrary presence in other people's lives and to honor complex worlds, both foreign and familiar, that I'd never truly considered. Feeling helpless and lost and dumber by the draft, I did my best to leave an accurate record of what resisted me, of all that I didn't understand, my little store of half-knowledge. Although I remember spending a long peaceful afternoon in the elegant hush of the Ryerson Library, reading books about brick, I rarely researched, preferring instead to work without a net—which may simply be another way of saying that I longed to fall. To fall, that is, and to hear what the descent had to say. "Bewilderment is the true comprehension," Luther wrote. "Not to know where you are going is the true knowledge." Truant in disposition, maybe I had no choice in the matter, but I took Luther's exhortation to heart, embracing it in the spirit of a possibility.

As a result, I've depended on my ignorance quite a bit, and maybe, just maybe, that gives the work a lopsided or eccentric shape and, at times, a certain velocity, a kind of venturi effect, as in an old carbureted engine, forcing the material through such a limited aperture of understanding—and I wouldn't want to gunk up the works with irritable facts and information gathered from Google.

Friends would diagnose me with a really bad, likely terminal case of aporia, but I suspect that my condition isn't so uncommon, that a little tribe of others feels, each in their own way, just as mystified and baffled as to direction as I do. At the risk of sounding parsonic, it seems to me we've ceded so much space to the expert and the confident authority that expressions of real doubt or honest ignorance are now regarded, in the demotic mind, as a kind of recreancy, a failure of loyalty, the sign of a faith betrayed. Our public space has become a matter of allegiances, always a prelude to ugly business, and as I worked on these pieces—stalled out, staring at the mess of contradictory notes tacked to my corkboard—I would wonder, in my uncertainty, where all the other people are who don't know, who don't understand. Are we—the hesitant, the conflicted—all alone? Can that be? In a leveling climate of summations, crowded with public figures who speak exclusively from positions of final authority, issuing an endless stream of conclusions, I get a wary sense in my gut of a world that's making its appeal to my indolence and emptiness, asking only for surrender. But when at last all of life is polled and made plural, when it's all been added up and averaged and answered and agreed upon, what happens if you don't feel so plural? In the face of so much decidedness I conceal my doubts in shame, or something of that character, feeling isolated and singular, useless and a little vulnerable, with all my innermost, urgent thoughts condemned to soliloquy. Cutting away what I consider the engine of the essay—doubt and the unknown, let's say—leaves us with articles and theses, facts and information, our side and their side, dreary optimism and even drearier pessimism, but nowhere to turn in a moment of true need. In that sense, I don't see any other option but to head west with Augustine; it seems not only possible but desirable that not-knowing would be the first condition of prayer. What I've collected here, of course, are just a bunch of scrappy incondite essays, not prayers, but behind each piece, animating every attempt, is the echo of a precarious faith, that we are more intimately bound to one another by our kindred doubts than our brave conclusions.

A small press published some of these pieces in a tiny volume called *Orphans*. This isn't the place to recount the saga of that ill-starred edition, but I'm happy to report that all thirty-five hundred copies of that feisty little foundling managed to find their vagrant way into the hands of readers, a solace to me like the thought of home. It was a small, small edition, easy to slip into a purse or pocket, and bears the distinction, I believe, of being sat on more than your average book. I've seen some really beat copies floating around, which serves me right. Thanks to Tin House, the substance of that book now lives on in this collection, reunited with some of its estranged siblings and joined by new work, including this gassy preface. Often the original titles were editorial decisions, hardly more than labels, and this time out, in *Loitering*, I've taken the liberty of rechristening the pieces, giving them the names they'll answer to for the rest of their lives. I've also attempted to structure the material, gathering certain unruly obsessions into familial groups, a task whose futility is somewhat akin to controlling a mudslide. The title of the book fits my sense of things nicely. Writing an essay is a form of loitering—a lingering, a skulking, a meandering—and I like the sinister undertone—*loitering with intent*—but in the end it brings me back full circle to that boy at the bus stop, reading in the dim light, and to all my brothers and sisters, whether by blood or by bond, who find themselves, now and then, without apparent purpose. ❖

PART 1:
WEST OF THE WEST

Austin: There's nothin' down here for me. There never was. When we were kids here it was different. There was a life here then. But now—I keep comin' down here thinkin' it's the fifties or somethin'. I keep finding myself getting off the freeway at familiar landmarks that turn out to be unfamiliar. On the way to appointments. Wandering down streets I thought I recognized that turn out to be replicas of streets I remember. Streets I misremember. Streets I can't tell if I lived on or saw in a postcard. Fields that don't even exist.

Lee: There's no point cryin' about that now.

—SAM SHEPARD, *True West*

Seattle, 1974

The initial salvos in my hankering to expatriate took the predictable route of firing snobby potshots at the local icons of culture, at Ivar with his hokey ukulele and Stan Boreson and Dick Balch with his ten-pound sledge, bashing cars and laughing like a maniac all through the late night, etc. (Actually, I thought Dick Balch was cool and so did a good many of my friends. He had the crude sinister good looks of a porn star and once merited an admiring squib in *Time*. In his cheap improvised commercials—interrupting roller derby and the antics of Joanie Weston, "the Blonde Amazon"—he'd beat brand-new cars with a hammer, so to me he always seemed superior to circumstance—our old cars just got beat to hell by life, whereas Dick Balch went out on the attack. It was a period when a lot of us hero-worshipped people who destroyed things, and even now I wonder where Dick Balch has gone and half hope he'll come back and smash more stuff.) Anyone born in geographical exile, anyone from the provinces, anyone for whom the movements of culture feel rumored, anyone like this grows up anxiously aware that all the innovative and vital events in the world happen Back East, like way back, like probably France, but before expatriation can be accomplished in fact it is rehearsed and performed in the head. You make yourself clever and scoffing, ironic, deracinated, cold and quick to despise. You import your enthusiasms from the past, other languages, traditions. You make the voyage first in the aisles of bookstores and libraries, in your feckless dreams. The books you love best feature people who ditched their homes in the hinterlands for scenes of richer glory. Pretty soon the word *Paris* takes on a numinous quality, and you know you won't be silent forever. Someday you'll leave.

Meanwhile, the only city I really knew was a dump worse than anything Julius Pierpont Patches (local TV clown) ever dreamed of, sunk in depression and completely off the cultural map, no matter what outlandish claims local boosters made for the region. And they made many. In a highly cherished book of mine (*You*

Can't Eat Mount Rainier! by William C. Speidel Jr.,
illustrated by Bob Cram, © 1955) I read, "What with
the city's leading professional men, artists, writers,
world travelers and visiting VIPs always dropping into
the place, [Ivar's] has become the spot where clams and
culture meet." Huh? Artists? Writers? To explain, Ivar's
is a local seafood restaurant, and Ivar himself was a
failed folksinger in the tradition of the Weavers. Back
then there was an abundance of clams and a paucity
of culture, but even more than this disparity, I'd somehow arranged it in my head that clams, salmon, steel-
head, and geoducks were actually antithetical to and
the sworn enemies of culture. No one wrote about
them, is what I probably meant. Perhaps clams and
culture met, once, in 1955, but then of course 1955
stubbornly persisted in Seattle until, like, 1980, and
in between time you felt stuck mostly with mollusks.
The culture side of the equation was most prominently
represented by a handful of aging rearguard cornballs.
Like Ivar himself.

If you were a certain type, and I was, you first had
to dismantle the local scene's paltry offerings and then
build up in its place a personal pantheon remote from
the very notion that clams and culture really ever do
meet, anywhere, at a time when, all arrogant and hostile and a budding prig, you believed culture was the

proprietary right of a few Parisians. That an old warbly-voiced yokel like Ivar might pass for culture, or that *Here Come the Brides* might signify to the world your sense of place, seemed a horror, an embarrassment. I went incognito; I developed alibis. For starters I took to wearing a black Basque beret and became otherwise ludicrously Francophile in my tastes. Mostly, however, I couldn't find solid purchase for my *snobisme*. Not that I didn't try. I'd have liked to be some old hincty Henry James but couldn't really sustain it. Still, you badly wanted things delocalized, just a little. Even if you had to do it first just in your head, with issueless irony. You looked about. With a skeptical eye you sized up the offerings. You wondered, for instance, why it was that suddenly in Seattle there was an aesthetic love of statues. You wondered, what is it with all these replicas of people around the region? A brass Ivar and his brass seagulls, some apparently homeless people (brass) in the courtyard of the Sedgwick James Building (as if a real, non-brass loiterer could actually rest awhile on those benches unmolested), and then, last, least, a hideous band of five or six citizens (cement) waiting for the bus in Fremont. Like a bunch of gargoyles walked off their ancient job guttering rain, they've been waiting for the bus twenty or thirty years now. If you've lived here long enough (like a week), you know the rain of today is the rain of tomorrow and the rain of a million years ago, and if you stand in that eternal rain long enough and often enough, you start to feel replicating the experience rubs it in your face. I've stood in the rain and waited for buses or whatever and it wasn't a joke, not that I understood, at least. You're standing there, you're buzzed, you're bored, you don't have a schedule, the rain's pounding around your head like nuthouse jibber-jabber, and from this incessant and everlasting misery someone else works up an instance of passing cleverness, then casts it in concrete for all time?

Those stone citizens, silent and forever waiting, are my nightmare.

I badly wanted to escape my unwritten city for a time and place already developed by words, for Paris or London or Berlin and a particular epoch as it existed in books. I wanted Culture, the uppercase sort. Books fit my minimum-wage budget and afforded the cheapest access. Fifty cents bought admission to the best. I purchased most of my early novels and poems from a woman who, I recall, had only one leg. Later there was Elliott Bay Book Company, which offered both a bookstore and a brick-walled garret in the basement. You could loiter without having to skulk. You could bring your empty cup to the register and ask for refills.

And you could read. Those books, more than any plane ticket, offered a way out. Admittedly it was a lonely prescription, an Rx that might better have been replaced by 100 mg of whatever tricyclic was cutting-edge back in the seventies. But who knew about such things? Instead I'd hide out in the basement of Elliott Bay or in the top floor of the Athenian and in my sporadic blue notebooks track a reading list—Joyce, Pound, Eliot, et al.—that was really little more than a syllabus for a course on exile. You could probably dismiss this as one of those charming agonies of late adolescence, but let me suggest that it's also a logical first step in developing an aesthetic, a reach toward historical beauty, the desire to join yourself to what's already been appreciated and admired. You want to find yourself in the flow of time, miraculously relieved of your irrelevance. For reasons both sensible and suspect, folks today are uneasy with the idea of a tradition, but the intellectual luxury of this stance wasn't available to me, and I saw the pursuit of historical beauty, the yearning for those higher essences other people had staked their lives on, as the hope for some kind of voice, a chance to join the chorus. I was mad for relevance, connection, some hint that I was not alone. I started scribbling in notebooks in part just so I'd have an excuse, a reason for sitting where I sat, an alibi for being by myself.

Seattle in the seventies was the nadir of just everything. A University of Washington prof. of mine, a
yam-faced veteran of SDS, inelegantly labeled us "the
phlegmatic generation." The word *apathy* got used an
awful lot. I quite sincerely believe Karen Ann Quinlan was the decade's sex symbol. Seeking an alchemic
dullness in quaaludes and alcohol, she actually found
apotheosis in a coma; that's what made her so sexy
(i.e., compelling) and symbolic to me. I'm not trying
to be ironic or waggish here. Objects restore a measure of silence to the world, and she was, for those ten
wordless years, an object. Her speechless plight seemed
resonant, delphic. The reason I remember her as such
an emblematic figure is that her coma coincided with
my own incognizant youth. The Seattle of that time
had a distinctly coma-like aspect and at night seemed
to contain in its great sleepy volume precisely one of
everything—one dog a-barking, one car a-cranking,
one door a-slamming, etc.—and then an extravagant,
unnecessary amount of nothing. Beaucoup nothing.
The kind of expansive, hardly differentiated, foggy
and final nothing you imagine a coma induces. I read
the silence as a kind of Nordic parsimony. An act of
middle-class thrift. A soporific seeded into the clouds.
All the decent dull blockheads were asleep, and you
could no more wake them to vivid life than you could

Karen Ann Quinlan. Being alone at night in Seattle began to seem horrifying; there was just so much nothing and so little of me.

You know how the story goes—I went away, I came back, blah blah. I now see the personal element in all this, the comic note, and I also realize the high European graft doesn't readily take to all American subjects. The predominant mental outlook of people I grew up with depended largely on a gargantuan isolation. When I finally went away I was always careful to tell people I was from Seattle, *Washington*, afraid they wouldn't know where the city was, which suggests the isolation of the place was permanently lodged in me. Finding myself at last in the warm heart of culture, in New York or Paris or even LA, I returned, like some kind of revanchist, to the cold silent topography I knew best, the landscape of my hurt soul. I first read Raymond Carver because in paging through his second collection at a bookstore I noticed a familiar place-name— Wenatchee—and latched onto the work solely based on that simple recognition. Ditto Ken Kesey. And then there was the discovery of Richard Hugo, a great epic namer, who beautifully described himself as "a wrong thing in a right world," and noted the oppressive quiet of the city the way I had, so that it seemed we were brothers, and offered to me a liberating emblem far better suited to my ambitions as a writer than a girl in a coma. These are probably just the humdrum dilemmas any writer encounters, and that I should express any keen pain at the difficulty of finding a subject and a voice is, I realize, kind of carping and obnoxious. It comes with the territory, after all.

And yet it is still some form of familiar silence that I struggle against when I write, something essential about the isolation. As Graham Greene wrote: "At that age one may fall irrevocably in love with failure, and success of any kind loses half its savour before it is experienced." For me the city is still inarticulate and dark and a place I call home because I'm in thrall to failure and to silence—I have a fidelity to it, an allegiance, which presents a strange dislocation now that Seattle's become the Valhalla of so many people's seeking. The idea of it as a locus of economic and scenic and cultural hope baffles me. It a little bit shocks me to realize my nephews and nieces are growing up in a place considered desirable. That will be their idea, rightly. That wasn't my idea at all. Vaguely groping for a diluted tertiary memory, people used to say to me, I've heard it's nice *out there*, and I'd say, Seattle has a really high suicide rate. (I was kind of an awkward conversationalist.) But really I didn't know if it was nice; it never occurred to me to wonder. I'd shyly shrug and mumble out of the conversation, saying I didn't know, it was home. Seattle does have a suicide rate a couple notches above the national average, and so does my family, and I guess that earns me the colors of some kind of native. I walk around, I try to check it out, this new world of hope and the good life, but in some part of my head it's forever 1974 and raining and I'm a kid and a man with a shopping cart full of kiped meat clatters down the sidewalk chased with sad enthusiasm by apron-wearing box boys who are really full-grown men recently pink-slipped at Boeing and now scabbing part-time at Safeway.

Today I go in search of an older city, a silent city. Early in the morning the painted signs on the buildings downtown seem to rise away from the brick in a kind of layered pentimento. The light at that hour comes at a certain angle and is gentle and noticeably slower and words gradually emerge from the walls. YOUR CREDIT IS GOOD. THE BEST IN RAIN GEAR. There is a place I can stand on Westlake Avenue and read the fading signs and recognize many of the names of people I grew up with. I've got my own people buried in the ground. I cross the Aurora Bridge and think special thoughts and know my brother's black Wellingtons are buried in the shifting toxic silt at the bottom of Lake Union. That brother's alive, and I thank God for certain kinds of failure. New silences layer over the old. I hope this brief superficial essay hasn't simply circled around a peculiar woundedness. Folks double my age and older often run down a conversation tracking a vanishing world that will, with the passing of their memory, vanish entirely. This is something more than benign senescent forgetfulness. So be it. Nowadays I feel like an old-timer in terms of estrangement. I don't know what determines meaning in the city any better than these old people with their attenuating memories. Probably traffic laws, the way we still agree to agree on the denotation of stop signs. I went away and in my absence other things have sprung up. Good things. It's a new place, but there's an old silence bothering me.

And now when I write I feel the silence pressuring the words just like the silence I felt as a kid, walking around town with nowhere to go. It used to be I'd wander down the alley around the corner from the Yankee Peddler and see if Floyd the Flowerman was in his shack. Floyd sold flowers out of a homemade shack, a lean-to patched together out of realtors' sandwich boards and such and propped up against what's now a soap shop, and he was a big fan of police scanners, of the mysteries of other people's misfortunes as they cackled over the airwaves and received, at least briefly, a specific locus, a definite coordinate within the city.

This oddball interest in fixing the detailed location of pain and disaster fascinated me. I'd say it prefigured the job of a writer, if the conceit weren't so obviously tidy. I can't now tell if Floyd was crazy. Probably he was just sixties jetsam, tossed overboard by the era and living like a kind of alley-cat Brautigan, "made lonely and strange by that Pacific Northwest of so many years ago, that dark rainy land . . ." That wet black alley, and then the queer miracle of his white shack, those flood-lit plaster buckets filled with red gladiolus, sunflowers, pink carnations, and then Floyd the hippie holdover tuning his scanner in to instances of tragedy, dialing up meaning and its shifting vectors.

One night when the bus just wouldn't come, Floyd and I walked in the rain down Stone Way to watch a house burn. He was very hepped up. The cold rain on our faces warmed to tear temperature in the heat of the burning house. I wish time would collapse so I could be watching flames and ash rise from that house and also see my brother falling through the air below the bridge. Obscurely I know this is a wish that Time, like a god, might visit us all in our moment of need. But Floyd's gone, and that brother's got a metal plate in his pelvis and walks a little funny, and myself, I wander around at night, taking long walks to clear my head before sitting down in front of my typewriter, walking for an hour or two as all the new and desirable good floats before me like things in a dream, out of reach, and I peer through the windows of new restaurants and new shops and see all the new people, but I don't go in, probably because I feel more in my element as the man who is out there standing in the rain or just passing by on his way home to write. ❖

Loitering

In the manner of the police blotter: On the night of July 8 a call was received saying a man was beating his girlfriend at 110 Vine Street in Belltown. Police responded and a hostage situation ensued. The man gave himself up, after an all-night standoff, at ten in the morning . . .

This is totally false, but for the sake of the story let's say the events in question begin around 2:00 AM, just because that's when I show up on the scene. The events as I find them are fairly meaty by big-league journalistic standards, involving domestic violence, assault and battery, a hostage, a gunman—all of which, I realize, could easily (and most often does) play itself out in lonely, tragic, and unobserved ways—but there's also, this night, cordons of yellow police ribbon closing off several blocks in Belltown, maybe fifty cops, a spooky antiterrorist vehicle the color of some nightmare rodent, plus a ruck of TV news reporters and their retinue of technicians. This guy— the Bad Guy—apparently thought he was just going to drink a few beers and bounce his girlfriend against the walls and go to sleep, but instead of a little quiet and intimate abuse before bed he's now got major civic apparatus marshaling for a siege outside his window. No sleep for him tonight, and no more secrets, either, not at this unholy intersection of anomie and big-time news. The story's been taken away from him, and other people are now trying to affect the plot. The police have a story they'd like to tell and so do the media folks and so, I suppose, do I, although in the hierarchy of things I suspect I'm just as clueless as the Bad Guy. When I arrive at First and Vine he's busy negotiating by phone. He wants to know what kind of trouble he's in.

The falling rain makes a pleasant hum on the asphalt, but barely a block away the whole city gives out, dissolved in a granular fog, and I dreamily sense that out there, out beyond the end of the avenues and streets where right now the only destination I see is murk, there might be silence again, a silence we might enter and lose ourselves in and thereby forget all this cowboy business of guns and women. Meanwhile, back in the real world, my first instinct is a sort of stupid ducking motion I've learned from the movies, and I have the sure sense I'm going to be shot in the neck, where I feel particularly exposed and vulnerable. At first I don't know in which building the guy's holed up, and I assume it's one of the high-rise Miami Beach–style architectural monstrosities that distort the human scale of this, the north end of Belltown. But this assumption is just pure cornball stuff, and I'm instantly aware that everything I feel and think is little more than the coalescence of certain clichés, that the Bad Guy isn't a madman barricaded in the top floor of the tallest building, that he doesn't necessarily plan to take potshots at pedestrians and commuters on their way to work, that he might just be drunk and deranged and wondering how he came to this strange pass on an ordinary evening that began normally enough and is now in the wee hours rapidly going to hell. In short, I don't know anything about him, beginning with the most fundamental thing, like where he is.

Not knowing where he is translates pretty soon into a polymorphous fear, and now it's not just my neck constricting, but also my shoulders and my stomach and my balls, the fear having spread practically right down to my toes as I vividly imagine all the places a bullet can enter the body, and I try to squat casually behind a cement wall—casually because I don't want to embarrass myself in front of the gathering pack of seasoned hardcore TV news journalists, who frankly seem, with all their unwieldy equipment and their lackadaisical milling around, like sitting ducks—until it occurs to me that the whole notion of being "behind" anything is a logistical matter I can't quite coordinate, since I don't know where the Bad Guy is. A ballistic line from point A (Bad Guy) to point B (author's neck) can't be established just yet, and for all I know I might actually be casually squatting right in front of him, cleanly fixed between his sights. In deer and elk hunting there's a moment when you sight your quarry, when everything is there, and you feel the weighty potential of the imminent second in your every nerve, and this weight, this sense of anticipation, this prolepsis, can really screw up your shot. It's as if the moment were vibrating, taking on static interference from the past and the future, and success depends on your ability to still it, to calm yourself through careful breathing right back into the singular present. The condition is variously called buck or bull fever, and I'm now feeling a variant of that, imagining myself notched neatly in the iron sights of the Bad Guy's gun. My fear is as vaporous and real and enveloping as the rain and fog, and I have this not-unfamiliar feeling of general and impending doom.

This might seem unnecessarily preambular, but I also want to say my pants are falling down and I'm sopping wet. I came back from salmon fishing in Alaska with a severe case of atopic dermatitis primarily caused by contact with neoprene. I had what's called an "id" reaction—pretty much systemic—and all week my fingers and neck and feet and legs were puffy and disgusting, with weeping sores. I think my condition even freaked the dermatologist. My hands were so raw and inflamed I wasn't able to type, hold a pen, or turn the pages of a book. Because I don't own a television my week of forced zombiism passed without distraction and nothing to gnaw on but my own increasingly desperate thoughts. I lay in bed, staring at the ceiling, the walls. It was a new kind of aloneness for me, being imprisoned in my own skin. It was easy to imagine never being touched by another human being ever again. The dermatitis made my skin crawl, and I was taking 40 mg of prednisone, a steroid that cruelly kept me awake so as, it seemed, to fully and consciously experience my suffering in a state of maximum alertness. I mention all this to establish a certain oblique connective tissue between observer and observed, between myself as witness and the thing witnessed. Half the reason I'm at the crime scene is I haven't had any human contact for a while, and besides I can't sleep with my skin prickling (and the other half of why I'm standing in the rain at two in the morning is I'm probably some kind of tragedy pervert). When I got back from Alaska my hands were already painfully suppurating and I couldn't carry all my bags and grabbed only the expensive stuff, the rods and reels, leaving a duffel of clothes in my truck. The next time I could put on shoes and walk, three days later, the neighborhood crackheads had stolen my clothes, including my only belt and my only raincoat, and that's why my drawers droop and I'm soaked and starting to shiver a little in this mellisonant humming rain.

But I didn't come to this crime-scene-in-progress innocently. Before leaving the apartment I put a pen in my pocket, along with a stack of three-by-five cards and a tape recorder, thinking that if this thing got real hairy, if there was actually some shooting, then I might jot a few notes and make of an otherwise blank night a bona fide journalistic story, full of who, what, where, when. Like a lot of my aspirations, this one, too, was internally doomed and hopeless long before I realized it. My main problem vis-à-vis journalism is I just don't have an instinct for what's important. I realize that now, looking over my notes. My first note was about the old alleys in Seattle, those island places where sticker bushes flourish and a man can still sleep on a patch of bare earth, where paths are worn like game trails and leave a trace of people's passing, and how these naturally surviving spots are systematically vanishing from the city, rooted up and paved over mostly because they house bums—an act of eradication that seems as emotionally mingy as putting pay slots on public toilets, but is probably cost-effective in terms of maintenance, since bums generate a lot of garbage in the form of broken glass and wet cardboard. Then I started another note about how, in contrast to these hardscrabble plots, the flower beds and parking strips of lush grass and manicured shrubs and trees are pampered and how, currently, it's maybe three in the morning and all up and down the street automatic sprinklers spit and hiss in the rain, redundantly watering.

Also my notes bleed black ink and blur in the rain as I write them. I don't write a note about that.

But after investigating the alley it occurs to me there's a whole parking lot full of highly paid professional journalists just loafing around and that some of them might answer a few questions. I'm not properly credentialed and I'm feeling a little timid because, with my falling-down pants, my soaking wet waxed-cotton coat, and my sore, swollen, hideous, raw red fingers, I don't look nearly so crisp and ready to report news as these people, and in fact, the way I look, I might be an escapee from the other side, I might just *be* a piece of news myself, but I need to approach them and find out what's going on and, if nothing else, I'd really like to fix on a location for the Bad Guy. Certainly these journalists know the scoop, otherwise they wouldn't look nearly so bored and unconcerned. Watching them from a distance, I have the feeling we're all waiting for dawn and that dawn, in turn, will bring us death; the atmosphere is straight out of an old Western, where the man gets hanged at sunup. I mean this whole aimless scene badly needs a plot, and nothing emphasizes that more than these journalists, these TV people, standing around in a parking lot scattered with expensive equipment that now waits idly for . . . *something*. All this inaction is underscored and made emphatic by the sheer number of journalists flocking in the lot, which creates a sense of collective anticipation, a weird hope. Really it would be a relief if that gun would go off.

In a kind of illustrated food chain of journalism there are big white vans representing every major TV station in Seattle and then several shrimpy economy cars, also white, with the names of radio stations printed on the doors. I notice every journalist is wearing a particularly nice raincoat, with team colors. Then I notice other things, like the cameras, the monitors, they too are covered in specially made rain bonnets. And a couple of people are walking around with umbrellas the size of parachutes. All these dry people are from another tribe. This kind of hard-hitting, high-level journalism obviously requires neat hair, which partly explains all the first-rate rain gear, and that equipment can't be cheap, not like three-by-five cards. One of the TV reporters is wearing navy-blue pants and a red coat, an outfit that resembles the unsexed uniform of a reservations clerk for a national hotel chain. Another TV guy is practicing a look of grave concern in his monitor, a look that, live at least, seems woefully constipated. It's weird to watch what amounts oxymoronically to a rehearsal of urgent news, especially without sound, emptied of content, because this pantomime of immediacy is patently fake, a charade, a fine-tuning, not of emotions, but the reenacted look of emotions. It's method acting or something. In a curious twist, I realize I always knew TV news *seemed* full of shit, but I never knew it was, in fact, full of shit. Previously I thought the TV news had a certain endemic phoniness because all the reporters were sorority girls who'd majored in communications, but it never occurred to me that the fakery was intentional. These people do this on purpose, and realizing that stunned me, because all my life I'd generously overlooked the canned quality of broadcast journalism, thinking it was, like other infirmities, something these people couldn't help. I thought they were just naturally corny people and no more deserving of scorn than cripples, and in fact were entitled, because of their impairment, to an extra helping of tolerance and understanding on my part. And now this morning I'm learning that that peculiar phony quality really is phony.

It's all big-time wrestling.

It occurs to me I'm not supple enough of an ironist to be alive and freely moving around in public anymore. With my skin practically leprous I might just hang a cowbell off my neck and clang around town the rest of my days.

I'm not going to mention the name of the big-league TV journalist I finally talked to because later in the morning, in between taping the twenty-five seconds of filler that feeds into the national show, he tried on a couple of occasions to pick up secretaries who'd come out on the sidewalk to gawk. Every time I turned around he was chatting up another secretary, then he'd rush in front of the camera and morph into the face of a slightly panicked and alarmed person nevertheless manfully maintaining heroic control while reporting nearby horrors. To look at his on-camera face you'd think Godzilla was eating lawyers off the Winslow ferry. It was clear to me that sometime in the past the putative luster of his job had landed him in bed with bystanders.

But before that, I thought he might be a reliable source of information.

"Hey," I said, "what do you think of this?"

"It's wet," the guy said, and then, I kid you not, he lit up a cigarette and squinted at the sky—just like a hero of some sort.

In a study of poetics you'd call that kind of rhetorical understatement *meiosis*. In its most simple metalogical form it works by deadpanning the ostensive situation (the Bad Guy with the gun, the hostage, homicidal intent) by rerouting it through the bluntly obvious and uninteresting observation that it is raining. This kind of locution can be found in *King Lear* and some of Auden's poetry, and it's nearly a national mental disease in England, plus it's pretty common in war, where the irony functions as an anodyne against other, more painful emotions.

Putting moves on secretaries, phony-faced reports, meiosis—you can't finally penetrate the pose to anything real.

I walk off and get my story by eavesdropping on a wondrously cute black woman wearing a blue coat, the back of which quite clearly states, in reflective block letters, her purpose: SEATTLE POLICE MEDIA RELATIONS. She's exactly what I've been looking for, maybe all my life. She's the unambiguous source of everybody else's story anyway. The most interesting thing I learn is there's no hostage.

"Is there a reporter here?" some guy demands to know.

His voice wavers with anger but his question floats unanswered and hangs ignored in a rude silence until, unnerved, I point to the parking lot and say, "Yeah, there's tons of them. They're all over the place."

Even as I watch the guy walk off I know in a low-frequency animal-to-animal way that he's the one, the man I need to talk to. Some part of this story is lodged inside him. In terms of clothing alone he's way worse off than I am, and what he's wearing, jeans and a T-shirt, show he's been rudely expelled from one cozy circumstance and dragged against his will into the rain. He's now caught in between, trapped in some place I recognize as life itself. It's obvious he hasn't been sober in hours and maybe years. If it could be said that these big-deal journalists have control of the story, and therefore, in a fundamental sense, are liars, albeit professional and highly compensated, then this guy is the anti-journalist, because in his case the story is steering him, shoving him around and blowing him willy-nilly down the street. The truth is just fucking with him and he's suffering narrative problems. He began the night with no intention of standing in this rain, and his exposure to it is pitiful. As he moves unheeded like the Ancient Mariner through the journalists I feel a certain brotherly sympathy for him, and I'm enamored of his utter lack of dignity. He's moved beyond all poses. I know he'll come back to me, that it's just a matter of a little more rejection, and when he returns, when he settles on me, I'll welcome him like a prodigal.

He doesn't know it yet, but I'm the only one who will listen to him.

Meanwhile we're at the edge of dawn, a first feathering of gray light that brings a bum stampede to the streets of Belltown. I live down here, and every morning at roughly five o'clock bums pour out of the missions and shelters and alleys in a kind of shabby and shadowy pre-commute, followed by the real thing an hour or two later. They pool up and briefly form a chorus. They fish around in squashed packs of GPC cigarettes, fire up. "Look at these news-media dicks," they say. Lights have come on in the IBEW Local 46 building and a few guys with lunch buckets are standing outside the Labor Temple Restaurant and Lounge. More and more people are standing around, trying to figure out what's going on. When the bums ask what's happening the question sounds yearningly metaphysical or like a child stirring from a dream. Their need to know, at any rate, is tonally different than that of a big-league journalist. And still we've got beaucoup reporters doing their insane pantomime of sincerity in the parking lot. It's like the Hitler tryouts in that Mel Brooks movie *The Producers*. None of the TV people have budged from their encampment in the parking lot, and I realize they're operating under the strictest criterion of relevance—every camera is focused in the same direction—and that their sense of the narrative is, generally, in sync with the police, that is, their reason for being here will end in a roughly coincident moment.

The guy's back. No one will listen to him, he's just learned.

"These fucking cops," he starts right up. "These goddamn pigs! They said there's no room on the bus. Me and my friend been standing in the rain all night. I'm a vet and he's an American Native. That ain't right. And these fucking assholes—you don't believe me? Here's my card."

He shows me his veterans ID, establishing his credentials, his suprapatriotic right to feel and also express his grievous outrage.

"That's some real shit," he says. "Dennis R. Burns. US Army Retired."

I tell him my first name.

"You know anybody?" he asks.

"You mean, like, somebody that could do something? Like Jesus Christ?"

"You a Born Again?"

"I was just joking."

"I know somebody," Dennis says.

I ask him if he knows what's going on.

"Yeah, got a guy with a gun, big black guy, 110 Vine Street, apartment #210. L. was throwing furniture at his girlfriend. This was about midnight. I'm the one that called the police, stupid me. I'm the maintenance man. L.'s generally a quiet guy, a little hypertensive, but nice. Very intelligent, well spoken."

"So he has a gun?"

"He's got two, a 9mm and something else, like a .357. I hope they don't hurt the man. Are you a journalist?"

"I'm really wet. You want some coffee?"

"What happened to your hands?"

"They're all fucked up. It's not contagious or anything."

"Are you a reporter?"

"Yeah," I say.

"7-Eleven's open. We could get coffee at 7-Eleven."

On the way there I pull out my Olympus Pearlcorder S803—*testing, one, two, three*—and discover the batteries are dead.

"You sure you're a journalist?" Dennis says. "Hey, my son's an editorial cartoonist for the *Albuquerque*

Times. He makes fun of everything—politicians, everything. He's always got a shitty fucking look on his face—like you."

On the way back from 7-Eleven with our coffees we hook up with Tom, who's drinking something throttled in a brown bag. He tells me, "I been up all night and I'm getting kinda moody. We were just gonna get drunk and listen to Elton John or some Asian music. But this gunman kept me up all night."

"And they wouldn't let us on the bus," Dennis says. And then he asks, "You ever write about Veterans Affairs?"

I feel bad I've led him on. "No," I say.

"There's prejudice on the bus," Tom says. "Those that like to drink and raise hell can't get on the bus. I tried to sleep on the sidewalk but it didn't feel right."

I ask about the gunman again.

Tom says, "I don't like L., but he's a human being. I live right above him and he's always yelling, 'I don't like white music!' I'm reservation Indian, but I'm part white too. I'm glad he's gone. He's gone now. He's not a tenant. Soon as he gives up, I mean."

I really want to know who the gunman is but certain elements of life in what's essentially an SRO conspire against the ready flow of this kind of information. In the main you're talking about people at the tail end of a trajectory, people who aren't any longer carrying around much of the baggage by which we're known to each other—family, jobs, schools, common aspirations, sundry memberships and affiliations, political grievances, etc.—and so asking for anything in the way of remotely biographical material brings scarcely more than vagaries. Dennis, for instance, insisted several times that the Bad Guy, L., was nice, a nice guy—but I don't get what kind of very elastic notion of "nice" he's talking about, given what's going on. And while of course everyone, even the most wrecked and destitute among us, has a unique personal history, the problematic nature of trying to gather information about people who've severed too many basic ties is this—that in a sense we truly have history only insofar as it's shared, and too much uniqueness really leads away from individuality to anonymity, the great sea of the forgotten. And because the Bad Guy is busy and I can't talk to him, I've got to rely on people who might reasonably be expected to know him, and in fact don't. I suppose it could also be said we're known to the extent that we're dull and orbital about our life, that what's quotidian about us is more easily shared than the exuberances and passions that push us out of the predictable.

And something like this is further confirmed when Dennis, Tom, and I arrive at the bus. Apparently the deal is that Metro brings around a bus for all the folks who've been forced to evacuate in situations like this, an ordinary accordion-style city bus where people can sleep and keep warm. Inside this bus what you see is pretty much a jackpot of social and psychic collapse, a demographic of bad news. Everybody in there's fucked up in some heavy way, dragged out of history by alcohol, drugs, mental illness, physical decrepitude, crime, old age, poverty, whatever. Riding this bus in your dreams would give you the heebie-jeebies big-time. There are maybe ten or fifteen people on the bus but between them if you counted you'd probably come up with only sixty teeth. In addition to dental trouble, there are people leaning on canes, people twitching and barefoot with yellow toenails curled like talons, gray-skinned people shivering in gauzy nightgowns, others who just tremble and stare. They've been ripped out of their bedrooms and are dressed mostly in nightwear, which is something to see—not because I have any fashion ideas or big thesis about nighties and pj's, but rather because, this surreal dawn, the harsh, isolated privacy of these people is literally being paraded in public. The falling rain, the bus going nowhere, the wrecked-up passengers dressed for sleep, the man with the gun—these are the wild and disparate components of a dream, and I haven't slept, and it's just weird.

And meantime that rodent-like anti-whatever vehicle has parked in the street below the Bad Guy's
window and there's a super highly trained SWAT guy
launching tear-gas canisters. We hear the dull pop
report like a distant shotgun blast, and then a rainy
sprinkling of broken glass on the sidewalk.

"There goes the windows," Dennis says. "Those are
double-pane, $145 apiece. I got a very secure job."

"Look how fast I left," Tom says. He pulls a TV remote control out of the pocket of his sweats and clicks
at the sky. "It's pitiful, I know. It's pitiful."

"What are the rooms like?" I ask, kind of trying to
figure the size of the rooms and calculate how fast the
pepper spray or tear gas or whatever will take effect.

Dennis says, "You got one room. You got a stove in
the room. You got a fridge in the room. You got a bed."

After I hear Dennis describe the Bad Guy's room,
the story, the night, everything, starts to end for me.
I know they haven't got him and maybe things will
go crazy an hour from now, two hours from now, and
people will die or some other TVish sort of scenario
will play itself out, but I don't care. I've been out here
for seven-plus hours and I'm really wet and can't hardly
bend my fingers anymore. My feet ache and swell inside my boots, even though I've removed the laces. But
that room! I'm starting to feel all buggy imagining that

man in that room. It sounds so simple, so stripped, so precariously close to nothing, yet outside all this complication is whirling around, cops and meter maids and a SWAT guy and a crisis negotiator and TV and spectators, everyone focused on this man in a room with a stove, a fridge, and a bed.

What would you do? How would you end this story?

I walk back to my place, change into dry pants, and feed the dog a bowl of kibble. I sit on the edge of my bed. To keep my feet from cracking I've bought a lot of fancy lotions, the labels of which make outlandish, existential promises. One offers itself as "cruelty-free"; another says it will rid my skin of the toxins that are an inescapable part of modern life. The thing is, over the last couple weeks my desire to believe has collapsed into actual belief, and I slather the stuff on like holy water at Lourdes.

I ease my feet into my boots and head back to First and Vine. In my mind I'm turning over the possibility that this whole strange night is a love story, and that if it is, if in fact there's some kind of romance at the heart of it all, then the entire event will elude me. Also I wonder, in an idle, academic way, why the police alone are so refreshingly without irony. Then I wonder why I find it refreshing. Then I think about the crackheads who stole my belt and raincoat and how the economics of addiction might connect up with this event. Then I go back to considering the love angle, how it's nearly impossible to convey our deepest passions yet damned easy to share what's dullest and worst about ourselves. I'm already composing the story in my head, but when I get back to First and Vine everyone's gone. The crime scene is no longer officially a scene because the yellow ribbon has been rolled up and taken away. The Bad Guy has surrendered. The police have left. The TV people are off on other assignments. Dennis is gone. Tom is gone. The bus is gone. The window is bashed to hell, the blinds mangled, but otherwise there's no sign of the siege and the night's dreamy drama; the workaday world is beginning and all of life is back to pumpkins and mice, and I feel like I'm just waking up, standing there on the sidewalk, all alone, loitering. ❖

Whaling Out West

The whale's belly is simply a womb big enough for an adult. There you are, in the dark, cushioned space that exactly fits you, with yards of blubber between you and reality . . .

—GEORGE ORWELL

Four in the morning and I crawl out of the tent, thinking, what's my penis for, anyway, other than pissing? Actually, as a man I've never been all that roosterly or priapic, so what I'm likely thinking about is not my penis but late itchy procreant urges and babies. Or maybe deep down what I'm really considering isn't babies but the worthless legacy of my carcass *in toto* and the way the Makah once used whale for drains, combs, toys, tools, oil, etc., for all that artifactual stuff in their fine, fine museum, and how flattered I'd be if my bones, my hair, my eyeballs, my skull and hide, if all my remains, now and at the hour of my death and the day after, meant the world to someone. What high praise to have your sacrum worked and whittled into scrimshaw and bric-a-brac or to have your occipital carved into a comb and drawn down through some lovely woman's long brown hair! Or merely to be remembered, to have told three pretty good jokes or made a funny face or cooked up a batch of pancakes in some kind of special way or done anything at all of lasting anecdotal quality. But none of that's likely in my case, when I go. Unless the gravedigger whistles a hymn as he works, probably no one'll even say a prayer.

I touch a stove-match to the mantle of my lantern and open the jet way up to full blast so its greenish light will beacon my way back to the tent, and then I dance on tiptoes through the fog and over the cold packed sand toward the sea. I've got to piss but have decided I want to stand in the Pacific Ocean, about up to my knees. The canker of self-consciousness has been long in me, so like a lot of writers I not only do a thing, I see myself doing it too—it's almost like not being alone. *That morning our hero skipped in his skivvies down to the shore of the sea . . . it was dark . . . the fog . . .*

Storytelling!

In fact the fog's so dense and obliterating, this pre-dawn offers a prospect as hopeless and unappealing as waking in heaven would after about the third day into eternity. And it is dark out, but kind of white-dark, like a chalkboard poorly erased. There's gooey sea lettuce and other kinds of kelp underfoot, and I can't really see. A wave washing around my ankles or perhaps a crease of white foam curling over in the sand will have to indicate a cautionary line where it's wise to stop or maybe not, maybe not, maybe walk on into the ocean, trust that the handful of people I haven't failed will remember me fondly, round things off right now and call it a life, make a biography out of this other-wise open aimless business.

Find closure!

One of Freud's disciples, Ferenczi I believe, devel-oped what was known as the thalassal theory, in which a man, in coitus, is supposedly trying via vigorous humping to shake loose or snap off his penis and send it forth in a sort of ambassadorial role, northward into the woman's womb, thus returning anadromously to his natal home.

Science!

Back inland my tent's a bright illumined bubble such as good witches might live in. Next to the Constitution and Baseball and the Roadside Billboard (loneliness in

space) and the All-Night Diner (loneliness in time), I'd
have to say the Coleman Lantern probably occupies
fifth place on my list of great American contributions
to civilization. No other lantern will do. The whisper
and hiss and cranky dyspeptic sputter of a Coleman is
as distinct and holy a music as the rev of a Harley. I like
the celestial quality of the light, Venusian and green,
the rounded simplicity of the mantle, the paint job, of
course, and the way one sounds when swung by the
bail. I've hauled the extra pounds of a Coleman up into
the mountains when it might have been more com-
monsensical to sit in the dark or scratch in my journal
by candlelight or bag words altogether and mindlessly
stare at the stars. And while I enjoy solitude I like as
much the convivial feeling of encampment in crowded
parks where families chatter and rehash fables and legends of the comical father while Coleman lanterns light
up and start the shadows of all the lovely mothers jitter-
bugging against the walls of trailers as they stow away
the hot dog buns.

This time out I'm alone, it's dark, but I haven't worried about the boogeyman in years; too often, though,
I've brought a case of troubled love out to this uncaring
coast. Dating way back, I can recall a catalog of poi-
gnancies. What's remained constant over the years is a
sense that when you're alone you're prey, or feel at least

it's potentially your fate to be stalked and eaten. Of course the benefits of being on your own include a certain vital spunk and a dexterity that comes to life when you're unencumbered, a spring in the step that keeps you ahead of the pack. Player and pep rally both, you cheer yourself on. Go! Yet everywhere beyond yourself is a bigness, a forest, a vault of stars, the surface of the sea, or the city at midday, ready to give you a drubbing. You vs. just about everything else. Alone, you're vastly outnumbered; but in the company of another, by some weird miracle of human math, the odds seem wonderfully improved in your favor.

Save the whales!

I have to confess I came out to this last, far corner of the country hoping to eat some whale. I came with the idea of getting a mathematically insignificant chunk of meat off a gray whale that washed ashore several years ago and was flensed on the beach and supposedly doled out by the Makah to every member of the tribe. It was like a roadkill whale, half of it necrosed and putrid and bound for the Neah Bay dump, half of it salvaged and stowed in freezers. This particular stranded whale maybe weighed twenty tons or forty thousand pounds (while the estimated number of extant grays currently stands at twenty-three thousand total, or by my loose estimates a whopping 1,702,000,000 pounds), and what I wanted was hardly more than a pork chop's worth of whale, maybe a pound, so that I might sample a tiny piece of the controversial behemoth myself. I just wanted to eat some. The Catholic in me thought eating a little leviathan—which I prayed would not in any way remind me of chicken, and which I suspected would taste like a petroleum product, say a bike tire or Vaseline—might bring me sacramental or at least alimentary insight. Foolishly I thought I'd just breeze into Neah Bay, pick up some whale, and flame-broil it for breakfast. I wasn't sure if whale was traditionally a breakfast food, but I'm not a Makah nor a student of indigenous peoples or aboriginal lifestyles, and I'm generally not inclined to go native, so anthropologic fidelity wasn't a big concern of mine. All I knew was I hoped to skewer and roast a piece of gray whale and feed the first honorary tidbit off this sort of cetacean shish kebab to my dog, experimentally, after which I thought I might even try it myself.

I packed in some stomach remedies in case I got lucky.

The supposed cuddly quality of cetaceans I just don't get. Between barnacles and sea lice, the few whales I've seen up close were hideously, hoarily disfigured or at least blemished and tactilely repellent the way certain so-called—not by me—pizza-faced teenagers are. I've seen stray grays in the Sound, come to shore to scratch their backs in Saratoga Passage, and they've all had a mottled gray pocked aspect, like poured cement. Their souls may be infinitely sweet and poetic, possessed of an earnestness and bonhomie I can only envy, but their bodies, in terms of color and surface texture, resemble bridge abutments. Not that these monsters shouldn't show a little wear and tear after making a yearly migration of 14,000 miles round-trip, so that, by the time the average gray is twenty, it's traveled 280,000 miles, or swum, basically, to the moon—which is truly awesome. It probably also explains that corroded crudded-up look. Gray whales get used roughly, making their migratory haul through Siberia, the Gulf of Alaska, etc., on their way south to the warm buoyant waters and calving grounds of Baja California. That's no frolic. That's a hell of a lot of use for any kind of carcass.

An encounter with a gray whale is bizarre, and if your first sighting happens unticketed and outside the enervated sanction of a tour, it'll seem contextually spooky and saurian. Gray whales don't look especially dirigible. You'd hate to have to park one. They have a lumpy crudeness of design, a banged-up body and a crimped ugly mouth and a dented snout, a color that seems to come from a supply of government surplus paint, and all around they have an unrefined and ancient and also untrustworthy aspect; they look like a mock-up of the kind of practice mammals God was making in the early days, before he hit his artistic stride and started turning out wolves and apes and chipmunks; and they've got that useless megaton bigness, a gigantism that's pretty dramatic in a circus-freak way or like other types of colossi or prodigies, the sheer extravagant enormity of which inspire sublime fascination or wonder or fear, but don't register much at the refined and fragile end of the emotional spectrum that includes the various colors of love or tender or chummy feelings of any sort. I myself can't square forty tons of whale flesh or even the word *blubber* with what I know about sweetness and intimacy; they're not ducklings or kittens or puppies or little lambs or fawns or piglets. In fact their very bulk seems inimical to closeness, to holding and embracing, but maybe, baby-freak that I've lately become, I can now conceive of love only in liftable forms, as something you put your arms around.

My numinous boyhood belief was that whales rose to the surface because they were lonely, tired of the depths. Their ancient bulk seemed to body forth exactly what it meant to be solitary, but breaching and spouting a sigh of relief through the blowhole in their head they lost some of their august self-sufficiency and were always depicted in familial groups, rather frolicsome and sweet, desirous of good company, of community. Obviously I was equating depth with darkness and darkness with cold and cold with silence and all of the above with a nearly insane state of isolation—OK, with my father—whereas things on the sunny maternal surface of *la mer* seemed to enjoy the sort of warm lapping buoyancy necessary for cultivating friendship and love. The story of Jonah reinforced this spatial arrangement, as did *Moby-Dick* later, where Pip sinks a fathom too far into the sea's immensity and comes up mad and/or mantic. But things have changed. Nowadays it's just as likely the surface of life is what puzzles Pip and finally sends him around the bend, and today's cabin boy must go alone into the quiet depths to escape and find peace and recover for himself a measure of sanity. It's civilization that's raw and wild and full of scary monsters and grotesques and deformities crowding every bus and park bench and court of law, and we now believe our wilderness exhibits the high sweet harmony we hope for from life as well as offering the refuge and sanative balm we desire when our energies flag and the botch of civilization gets us down.

Paul Watson's floating around somewhere out there in the very same fog as I am, Captain Paul Watson of the Sea Shepherd Conservation Society. He seems to have commandeered the environmentalist argument— and there's a creepy uncritical parroted quality to what everybody else in the pro-whale (or is it anti-Indian?) camp is saying—and his main, openly stated fear (as opposed to his real agenda, of which, more later) seems to be the precedent the Makah hunt will set for other whaling nations. But if the problem really is the recrudescence of commercial whaling and wide-scale industrial slaughter, then the Japanese ought to be taken to task for their rapine, or the Norwegians, or whomever, but it's a pretty specious argument that can make the corruptions and failures of these people somehow the direct fault of the Makahs. It's a sophistic argument, in fact, but Paul Watson's not much of a logician; he's mostly a misanthrope and a sentimentalist (how often those things go together!), sweet on whales and sick about what he calls "base-virtued" humans, and his rock-ribbed stance re: the hunt is all about the lone whale, soulful and solitary, perhaps a poet, singing songs, echolocating down the coast, intelligent, gentle, sentient, loving, unfairly ambuscaded (by heathens!) while going about its business—pretty much the otherworldly and animistic whale of my boyhood.

There's not now nor was there probably ever a shortage of love for Indians in the noble and rhetorical abstract, but even more abundant and pressing has been a heap-big annoyance at the nuisance created by Injuns who are actually alive and walking around and scratching their bellies and grumbling about what's for dinner or listening to the radio or reading books or arguing over the rules of Monopoly and especially those who are rather clamorous (uppity) about their needs. It all gets so queer and drifty and hard to track these days. Eco-Elements on First Ave. downtown has been instrumental in gathering signatures for a petition against the Makah, and it's one of those New Age emporiums with a syncretic, boutiquey approach to spirituality, a sort of travel agency specializing in tourism for the soul, emphasizing past lives, future lives, every kind of life but the really incompliant and unruly present, where tarot, runes, goddess-stuff, astrology, Native American spiritual resources, healing soaps and oils and aromas, candles that calm you down and bells that strike a special, particularly resonant and congenial note—where all this totally creeps out the stodgy Pauline Catholic in me, and yet—yet!—this reaching out to the arcane holy world, this Luddism of the soul, however fey and preposterous and apostatic and pagan it might seem in my eyes—you'd think this grab bag of atavistic practices would put the New Ageists in deep and direct sympathy with the Makah.

But it doesn't. And not so weirdly, a lot of the attacks on the Makah seem to gut and hollow out the "Indian" and take that rhetorical material and use it as stuffing, which in turn is packed into whales. The clichés about Indians transfer easily into clichés about whales, similar in substance and similarly hackneyed, yet housed in different vessels. The noble savage qua noble mammal. This can't be flattering to the Makah, while I imagine metaphor in general is probably a matter of oceanic indifference to even the most poetic gray whale. And the rhetorical violence—the stealing of language, the silencing—shouldn't surprise anyone even remotely versant with white/Indian history. Captain Watson likes to footnote his superior credentials as an Indian enthusiast from way back—Wounded Knee!—and yet somehow without tearing his brain in half he's able to plunge ahead with low, vicious, even paranoid attacks on the Makah as people. A small measured dose of irony should prevent this kind of mental sloppiness, but doesn't, probably because people in the environmental movement, like holy folks everywhere, don't make real keen ironists. I can pretty well guess that these sort of merit-badge Indians aren't entirely or enthusiastically embraced by your average enrolled tribal member, especially as they listen to Watson float pseudo-arguments that asperse the character of the Makah and accuse them of being liars, frauds, cheats, racketeers, colluders, and, of all things, fake Indians.

Abstract love is the nosy neighbor of abstract hate; they see right into each other's windows and they always agree on everything. And neither one of them really tests disinterestedness, the ability to make tragic choices between things of equal worthiness and legitimacy—which to my mind explains why so much writing and discussion about whales tends toward melodrama, where right and wrong are always clear, where only one of the terms is justified. "The opposition are not nice guys," Captain Watson has written. Nice? That seems a simpy word for a big old jackpot of a problem, a lazy and sinister trope suggesting that to oppose (Paul Watson) is to lack niceness, by definition. "I have no time for the arguments of tradition," Watson, the honorary Indian, has written. And further: "I have no wish to understand them. I have no wish to argue the pros and cons of whaling." He says, "The tradition of whalekind is of far more value to me." And this tradition comprises what? "They [the whales] grace the azure blue with a majestic intelligence wedded to an amazing tactile grace. A profound, elusive, ephemeral sentience, they deify the abysmal depths with their regal presence." If you can love abstractly, you're only a bad day away from hating abstractly. Somehow mere difference has been torqued up and given a moral dimension; by way of solution we know the next step—wearying to think of as another century wanes away—is to call for the annihilation of all distinctions.

The real high-ass muck-a-mucks of the pro-whale debate like to think they cut somewhat quixotic figures, noble, paladin, but the environmental movement in the matter of the whale hunt hasn't represented the best thinking by the best people; it's been a disaffecting display, at least for me. Where are the eloquent American saints, where is Thoreau, where Emerson, Muir, Marshall, Leopold, Olson, Abbey? Even David Brower, for God's sake! It's too bad Watson's so blinkered because the man knows cetaceans, as a student of the species and a hands-on advocate, better than anyone. He sees the situation, globally. His knowledge of whales is compendious and compassionate, but in public, dealing with people, he comes off as a bullying prig—his manners on the talk show *Town Meeting* were particularly appalling. With broader vision—a vision that extends to people even an ounce of the generosity he lavishes on whales—he might really help sort this mess out. He might even be able to broker a deal. He could wangle concessions. But Watson seems paranoid whenever he's writing about whales; in one astonishing sort of Christic psychomachy (*Sea Shepherd Log*, spring 1997) he relates the tale of his conversion, his Damascus experience, his baptism in whale blood, and puts himself across as a persecuted man, a prophet and savior. This messianic aspect of the movement, its higher, holier purity, is hard to stomach. It's theocratic and imperial and arrogant, and because of it Watson comes across as just another flawed man and broken reformer hiding his human failings behind another lofty and immaculate and inviolate cause.

The acronymic groups—PAWS, AFA, SSCS, PETA, etc.— who've organized opposition to the Makah hunt don't go for killing sea mammals under any circumstances. That's really their stance, and, boiled long enough, the irreducible core of their case. This intractability has lent a sullen and futile feel to the debate, a mudslinging, lie-swapping, smug, accusational tone that, rather than clearing the air, actually just fouls and debases anybody and everybody who joins in. These people have made up their minds; there's never been any room to maneuver. They're into whales, and not real fond of humans. In fact they seem to favor any of God's creatures over the malignant cancer of humanity. Their misanthropy takes the metaphoric exuberances of the late odd brilliant crank Edward Abbey literally, which is always scary. I mean, from Christ to Nietzsche we know it's one thing when the rich voice of a solitary radical shouts out and it's another thing when the echo of the ochlocratic chorus comes roaring back in agreement. Suddenly a certain kind of valence is gone. Abbey was a philosopher, wit, pisser, and prose stylist, and one of the first qualities sacrificed by his adherents is the anarchic soul of a man who claimed the Peace Corps was a "piece of insolence," "an act of cultural arrogance." The kind of man who could litter and make the act seem deductive, radical, and exemplary. The kind of man who strongly advocated population control and yet fathered four children himself—but by five wives, he argued, which was, when you did the math, only 0.8 children per woman, well below the national average. But when the lesser souls pick up the program, they smooth out the saving contradictions, flatten the subtleties, excise the humor, empurple the prose, hoist the flag and recite the pledge, and then march forth like fanatics and disciples and crusaders everywhere, ready for jihad and genocide.

Watson's been assigned the task of interpreting the psychograms sent to him by whales and apparently he's heard from the whales that they'd rather not be harpooned. His stated claim is that he'd like to return whales to some state pre-everything—Eden, the womb—while the Makah in an obvious clash would in some measure like to return themselves to a pre-contact world, before Captain Vancouver, before Puget, Rainier, etc., and certainly before Captain Paul Watson showed up on the scene.

Myself, I really doubt the efficacy of the Makah project because generally I'm skeptical about movements to restore culture. Whether the project's conducted by Hitler or Mussolini, Yukio Mishima or Ronald Reagan, or fundamentalists in Iran, Libya, or Idaho, or by Wovoka and the Ghost Dancers, or by modern communicants who raise their heads heavenward to receive the body and blood, I just don't think the hoped-for resurrection or the dream of a return to glory is viable. Randall Jarrell once wrote that even in the Golden Age people were always griping about how everything looked yellow; all our hopes elude us. Just as shadows fall across lives, history falls across cultures. Things unravel never to reknit again and contact quite likely brings with it the entropic doom Levi-Strauss talks about in *Tristes Tropiques*. Our complex intermingling kills. We wake out of our dreams and wonder where the blood on our hands came from. Knowledge happens just about as often as shit, while innocence is probably returned to by taking yet another bite of the apple, not by pretending there never was a Fall in the first place.

But my despairs are Western despairs and I really don't know a thing about the restorative capacity of the Makah soul.

Regardless, right or wrong, it's not up to me to judge the eventual cultural outcome for the Makah of killing a whale off the coast, and not because I'm indifferent to the fate of the environment, or because I agree or disagree with what the sloganeers for either side have to say about whales, but because the Makah are an independent people who ought to be able, for once, to fail on their own, without the encouragement of white folk. Or, vice versa, sort of, they ought to be allowed the chance to succeed without a boost from the BIA, HUD, HIS, Department of the Interior, missionaries, social workers, tourists, etc., on terms they've developed by and for themselves. They might like for once to be free of the entangled bureaucracy of being Indian. Or they might like to paint their asses green and play hacky sack by moonlight. I don't know. I can't say. The intestine affairs of the Makah don't really interest me, although I'm certain within the community there are factions, pro and con and even indifferent, but probably what's not needed now is a lot of high-minded refereeing from the outside. They have a treaty, and really the hunting of this whale is about our honor. We need to think about ourselves.

Killing a whale the Makah way is a highly specialized undertaking, and I can't imagine anyone doing it for kicks or as a show of bravado or even as an incautious stab at reviving culture. There are other ways to go about getting your daily bread, most of them drier and warmer.

At the Makah Museum there are a couple of bow and arrow sets but they're really pathetic-looking and I thought, seeing those flimsy toys, man, it's a pretty good bet these Makah didn't eat a whole lot of bear meat. The arrows were hardly longer or stouter than hot dog sticks; the bows didn't seem flexible or tensile enough to generate enough velocity to puncture hide, let alone find the heart of a bull elk from forty feet. But then you walked around and saw the whale and seal harpoons and the massive halibut hooks and the fishnet ingeniously fabricated from nettles—nettles!— and you realized that here was the sphere where these people really kicked ass.

Even in the long-gone Ozette olden days, five centuries ago, they had little baby harpoons for kids to play with, complete with mini-fingerholds, a kind of bridge or granny stick crotched for launching harpoons, so these little Makah boys would get the exact right feel of the weapon and begin to perfect their stroke from the moment they reared back and stuck their very first—I don't know—tree stump. What little Willie Mayses developed their form and a sense of the world's exact rightness playing with these sticks on the sand-lot beaches of what's now the Makah Nation? And the big-league harpoons their daddies used —what fantastic inventiveness it must have taken to figure out the logistical details of that first hunt, what holy-making number of Makah bones are buried and scattered beneath the sea around Cape Flattery, what lives were lost, what women cried, what children wondered, what brothers went silent, while these men worked out the kinks in their whale-killing prowess. Some amazing man, some Moses of the Makah, had to have had a vision powerful enough to lure and lead the others on. That magical moment alone should be saved from extinction. Think on it—you take the biggest body of water in the world, and it's the edge of winter, it's maybe lonely and horrifying and you're melancholic in some affective-disordered way and all around you there's an extra-heavy-duty cobalt rain battering down, and there at your feet on the beach you've got a pile of old bones and a couple of tree branches and somehow, looking at them, and looking out to sea, somebody comes up with the idea of sticking a thirty-ton whale? It stuns the mind, it blasts and levels the imagination.

Up to my knees in nature, I get mighty cold, naturally. I shiver in paroxysmal fits and feel what's possibly the onset of hypothermic derangement, and so I head back to the tent, dry off, do ten jumping jacks, then ten more, pull on a pair of clammy jeans and a fleece jacket and a goofy crushed duck-cloth cap I favor in the fall, and start a fire. Twigs and bark and moss and a few credit card receipts to kindle the flame, larger sticks of driftwood propped tepee-style to keep it going. As I work and warm myself the sky lightens from one shade of unhopeful gray to another. I collected and chopped wood half the night, hoping to exhaust myself and hold bad thoughts at bay. It didn't work. Poise and stability are not about never moving but rather about nimbly keeping step with the world as it pitches and rolls below your feet—one of several Hallmark-isms I try to live by.

When I go to feed the dog I find I've forgotten to bring her bowl; I pull off my cap and fill that with kibble. The waxed cotton holds water nearly as well as it repels it and she laps up a cool hatful after eating. I smack the hat against my thigh and set it back on my head. For entertainment and edification I've got *Field Guide to North American Weather* and Pascal's *Pensées*, but right now I'm not in the mood to sit in the fog and read about fog, nor do I, feeling skeptical and doubt-ridden, much care to read what the brilliant transit planner has to say about skepticism and doubt.

My mood? Fuck the whales! This too is nature—all of it, and maybe when I get back to Seattle I'll place a personal in the *Weekly*, truthfully saying, like most do, that I'm into nature, the woods and long walks, red wine and fires and poetry, philosophizing and fucking, the dawn light and the starry night, and all the other inadequate and hugely depressing analogues for unique and heightened sensitivity.

The real tragedy in this state isn't the healthy run of migratory whales that hug the coast in October/November but the passing of the salmon, the magnitude of which is equivalent in scale to the disappearance of sixty million buffalo from the plains in one short murderous span of the nineteenth century. Fewer and fewer people in the region have any memory of real, living salmon and seem satisfied with the bullshit touristy display of tossed fish at the market, and so nothing will ever actually be done and those coho and kings—kings! Tyees!—are gone and gone, it's horrible to say, with a whimper. No single salmon is big enough to be a cause célèbre on its own, whereas one whale the size of a Winnebago is, and so people notice. And, noticing, they get all drippy about whales, remotely enlivened and stirred to abstract opinion, when, in fact, the loss of salmon should rouse them to enormous, cetacean-sized outrage, and doesn't, since who cares where it comes from—salmon raised on farms! in frog ponds!—as long as filets and steaks of it are still served on plates around the city? Nary a salmon fighting to spawn in your local stream, but down the street there are plenty cooling on beds of ice behind the local grocer's display case.

I had no luck getting any whale. I asked. I did. I made phone calls and inquired at the museum and stopped strangers on the street and said to my waitress at the diner, you don't have any whale, do you? I even checked the freezer section of the grocery store. Along the way many, many Indians—men, women, and children; the old and the young; workers and loafers; thin, fat, tall, and short; braided and shaved—laughed right in my face. They weren't unduly snickering or snide about it; generally the laughter was big, hearty, frank, and guffawish. They seemed to find in my question a new comical low point, even after months of talking to journalists.

No whale—so the meager larder I laid in for this trip includes a supply of Wellbutrin, Mylanta, ground coffee, a gallon of fresh water, a package of Hostess cupcakes, kibble for my dog Kala, and a fresh filet of salmon off a small resident silver I caught in the Sound the day before.

Communion

we worship
the salmon

because we
eat salmon

—Sherman Alexie

I prop open the hood of my truck, pull out the dipstick, burn the excess oil off in the fire, and skewer
my salmon by interlacing four or five clumsy sutures
through the skin. (Better prepared, I would've baked
a few potatoes on the engine manifold. A woman in
Montana told me I should always keep a can of black
pepper in my tool kit, because in a pinch it'll plug a
radiator leak. When I asked her if there were any other
spices I ought to store in the car, she said an onion
in your glove box isn't a bad idea for your DUI situations. Had I heeded her advice, my truck would've
been pretty much as fully equipped as my kitchen.)
Anyway, I get my unadorned filet sizzling over the fire
and the skin instantly starts dripping gobbets of crack-
ling fat on the coals. I set some coffee on my stove
and crank the flame. I lean back against a log and look

at my watch, angling the face into the firelight. It's a quarter to five.

The men in my family have undone themselves in some kind of grand westering impulse gone awry. We ran out of land and then went one step farther, west of the West. We've shot ourselves and jumped from bridges and lost our minds and aborted some of our babies and orphaned others, and now reproducing and carrying on the family name is down to me, and the truth is soul-wise I'm likely a bigger monster than either of my broken brothers or my father. As the extant capable male in my family I either perpetuate our name or wipe it off the earth forever. The hints about what I should do haven't been so awfully subtle that even a mental clodhopper like myself can't catch the drift. Nature in me has come up empty, and so be it. I figure it took thousands of years to make Irish and Italians of my grandparents; America undid that in a scant generation. We've come to nothing—so soon?

Shine On, Perishing Republic!

I'm not sure I want to be the dead end of it all but then again how would I really feel with my seed trailing after me, wanting things? The mythopoeia of my family now seems to say if we persist in any patronymic way that's history and destiny and if we die off then in some loop-the-loop of logic that turns out to be history and destiny as well, ha ha.

It's always been a fond Western dream, after all the blood and pavement and franchising, to undo the whole sorry business and begin again.

The first best seller in America was an epic poem by Michael Wigglesworth called *The Day of Doom.*

There's a beginning.

What's left to say?

I wish I had some children that were around going, "Daddy, Daddy," so I could provide a wise impartial answer or at least pour a glass of milk for them. Who needs Pascal—"When I consider the short duration of my life, swallowed up in the eternity before and after, the little space which I fill, and even can see, engulfed in the infinite immensity of spaces of which I am ignorant, and which know me not, I am frightened, and am astonished at being here rather than there; for there is no reason why here rather than there, why now rather than then"—since even without a philosophical assist my uselessness appalls me.

The fog's gone away like a ghost. I turn off my lantern. I pick my salmon off the dipstick and eat it with my fingers and watch to the south as a great confetti-ish flight of seagulls spins through the air; and behind me a sandhill crane with an ungainly pterodactyl *whomp* of its wings lifts above the estuary of a river whose name I don't know; once aloft on its six-foot wings the crane soars in a circle with unlabored grace, landing back in the alluvial mud exactly where it began.

Where am I, in what land, in whose time?

Right this moment in the matter of Here vs. There I guess I'd rather be in some warm kitchen with little pieces of dirty chicken on the linoleum and last night's macaroni noodles underfoot and a pile of unwashed bobbies in the sink. And just exactly where are all the fine, tender, decent, steady, productive, forthright family men in the world right now, men toward whom, in infrequent but fairly rhythmic, practically menstrual fits of waking horror, I feel jealous? Not on this beach, that's for sure. I guess my true Here will always be an Elsewhere. And so I've arrived in this strange place and it's OK for now, it's rich, it's really queer, it's made of the morning a kind of phantasmagoria, the stuff of dreams and fevers, and what was I really thinking anyway, that my phantom children, needing wisdom and milk, were supposed to be out here with me, pissing in the ocean too? ❖

Catching Out

My father's agoraphobia made leaving the house a spooky and ritualistic process, ruled by mysterious tempers, but with enough drugs it sometimes happened, and we were off, the whole family, on vacation! The drugs that loosened his nerves and made the big bad outside world navigable also made him a sloppy driver, weaving lackadaisically around the highway, and wherever we were going—California, Vancouver—would seem very far away. Invariably, our crappy car would catch fire on steep grades (my sister's job was to douse the transmission hump with water when she saw the carpet fibers smoldering), plus with seven kids, all piled on top of each other, somebody was always carsick and ralphing in the backseat. We kept an old dented saucepan in the car, called the Spit-Up Pan, which we passed around so my dad wouldn't have to pull over every time a child needed to vomit.

Subsequently, I've never been much of a vacationer, and even now, when somebody starts talking about Hawaii or Cancun or St. Barts, I pray they won't mention the color of the water and tell me about snorkeling. As a young man, I tried Europe, but the woman I was meeting, on our second day in Paris, said she needed time alone, and went off to Barcelona with somebody else. For three days I walked to the Hôtel de Ville for reasons that are too stupid to admit and read an omnibus edition of Dashiell Hammett. I'd never been lied to like that, and I took my pain to mean I lacked continental sophistication, and Paris sort of died inside me.

But!

I loved hopping freight trains. It was cheap, dirty, loud, picturesque, illegal, athletic, dangerous, and, best of all, it didn't seem like a vacation. In fact, as far as I could tell, judging from personal experience, as well as things I'd heard, there was nothing in riding trains that even remotely resembled pleasure. It was hard work. You walked for miles on a crippling ballast of gravel, looking for an open boxcar, and slept on a cushion of cardboard, your feet forward, in the direction of travel, so that you wouldn't break your neck in a derailment.

You drank water from old Clorox bottles. You pissed out the door. You ate canned sardines. The schedule was indifferent to your needs and the destinations were all pointless. The only souvenir I have from that time is a rusted railroad spike. There might have been some romance to it—there might have been some road signs and red neon, some dead ends and diners, some hash browns—but really I was just skylarking. All the skills necessary for hopping trains were the sort you master by the time you get out of grade school. It was all jungle-gym stuff, it was monkey bars and rings and ladders, and if you could climb and run, if you had reasonable balance, if you liked jumping and bouncing and falling, then you could ride freight trains.

The minute you entered a yard the bigness of the trains translated right into your bones. I know it sounds corny, but you got proxy thrills of power, wandering around in those corridors made from some of the world's big machines. It was jarring to be in their midst, they were so gargantuan. Boxcars wide as whales, locomotives roaming up and down the yard with the single white eye of a Cyclops, grain hoppers overflowing with corn and wheat, gondolas piled with scrap metal and flatbeds loaded with raw logs or finished lumber, triple-deckers packed with import cars, empty deadheads and old rusting crummies shunted onto sidings. The dreamy size of the trains made your sense of trespass keen— it felt fatal—and the noise of the yard was enough to knock you over. And yet for all the vagrant time I spent, I never had any real hassles. The guys who work the trains are among that peculiar class of impassioned men in America, men who love their work and, loving it, want to share, as though they were holding their job in trust and some fabled and crucial part of America were stored inside their days in office. They're like firemen in that respect, without the tiresome noble sentiments. I'd wave collegially to the brakemen high up in the cupola of a caboose and talk easily to the men making up trains, men who in turn would pull a manifest from their pockets and point out a decent ride, an empty box or gon on the next train out.

Boxcars were the best rides, offering a room with a view and some protection from the rain or sun or snow, a leeward wall out of the wind, a dark corner to hide in when the snakes who walked the line came by, checking hydraulics. I'd jam a stick or discarded brake shoe in the door so it wouldn't rattle shut and make a sepulchre of the box while I slept. Most nights, though, I stayed up late, sleepless, because of all the bouncing, and besides, I liked the clangor of crossing guards, candy-striped and flashing with warning lights, an idled car or two waiting in the dim red glow.

After a few days you were filthy, carrying a funeral around on your face. The dirt wasn't unpleasant and mostly I remember feeling it was honorable—I translated it directly into miles, into small towns and states. I would pack along a pair of gloves, which kept my hands somewhat clean as I climbed over couplings and boosted myself into boxcars, but in the main I liked being dirty and feeling, on some level, strange and unwelcome. It sharpened my longing and called upon reserves of faith I didn't know I possessed. The dirt was like an account, a measure of wealth, and so, as the days and miles went by, I felt as though I were becoming someone. ❖

This Is Living

I was seven and had a leather purse full of silver dollars, both of which, the purse and the coins, I considered valuable. I wanted them stored in the bank. At the time, the bank had an imposing landmark status in my map of the world, in part because it shared the same red brick as the public school, the two most substantial buildings in our town. As a Catholic school kid I did a lot of fundraising in the form of selling candy bars, Christmas stamps and fruitcakes, and my favorite spot for doing business was outside the bank, on Friday afternoons, because that was payday. Working men came to deposit their checks and left the bank with a little cash for the weekend. Today, that ritual is nearly gone, its rhythms broken, except for people on welfare, who still visit banks and pack into lines, waiting for tellers, the first of every month. But back then I'd set my box of candy on the sidewalk and greet customers, holding the door for them like a bellhop. Friends of mine with an entirely different outlook on life tried to sell their candy at the grocery store, but I figured that outside the supermarket people might lie or make excuses, claiming to be broke; but not here, not at the bank, for reasons that seemed obvious to me: this was the headquarters of money. Most of the men were feeling flush and optimistic, flush because they were getting paid and would soon have money in their pockets, optimistic because the workweek was over and they could forget what they had done for the money. On their way in I'd ask if they wanted to buy a candy bar and they'd dip a nod and smile and say with a jaunty promissory confidence that I should catch them on the way out. And I did. I sold candy bars like a fiend. Year after year, I won the plastic Virgin Marys and Crucifixes and laminated holy cards that were given away as gifts to the most enterprising sales-kids at school. I liked the whole arrangement. On those Friday afternoons and early evenings, I always dressed in my salt-and-pepper corduroy pants and saddle shoes and green cardigan, a school uniform that I believed made me as recognizable to the world as a priest in his soutane, and I remember feeling righteous, an acolyte doing God's work, or the Church's. Money touched everyone in town, quaintly humanizing them, and I enjoyed standing outside the bank, at the center of civic life. This was my early education into the idea of money.

My hand will always remember the density of those silver dollars, the dead weight as I tumbled them back and forth, the dull clink as the coins touched. The nature of that weight offered a lesson in value too; you knew by a sense of the coin's unique inner gravity that the silver was pure, that it wasn't an alloy. Holding the coin in your palm you felt the primitive allure of the metal itself, its truth. Years later, I would pay for college by fixing washing machines and dryers. I was a repairman for a company that installed coin-operated machines in apartment buildings and laundromats. We had collectors in the field, men who worked set routes, hitting laundry rooms all over the city, emptying the coin boxes into canvas sacks. Late in the afternoon they returned to the shop and delivered the dirty bags to the counting room. The coins were filthy, turning everything they touched the lugubrious gray of pencil lead (you see the same graphite stain on the fingertips of people who play slot machines compulsively). The counting room was a dingy, windowless, fortified cement vault in back of the repair shop. Inside was a conveyor belt and a slotted metal chute and a machine for sorting the coins. A woman named Laurel did all the counting. She was thin and pale and her hair was limp and she wore black-rimmed glasses and a flowered smock that seemed a peculiarly sad flourish in that colorless place. She was a drudge in the operation, and unconsciously I equated her plain looks with honesty, her weak sexual presence with a lack of guile. Every afternoon thousands of dollars worth of coins slid across her tray. The metallic droning of the coins was mind numbing, and yet this woman, hearing the slightest deviation in that monotony, would toggle a switch and stop the belt, poke through the money in the chute, and pluck out the one silver coin—a Mercury dime, or a Washington quarter that predated copper-nickel composition—and replace it with one of her own. Thus in a matter of seconds she would make between a hundred and a thousand percent on her investment. One day she invited me into the counting room and demonstrated all of this, tapping a quarter against the tray, trying to teach me the subtle difference between the sound of a standard and a silver coin, and I never thought of her the same afterwards. The racket of those rattling coins was hellish in the confinement of her concrete bunker, but this pallid, dreary woman had a keen ear for that one true thing, the soft dull sound of silver as it thunked against metal, and she would eventually amass a small fortune in rare and valuable coins.

My silver dollars felt like a fortune, assembled and protected and given value by an abiding faith, a loyalty to them. They were Christmas gifts from my father, one for every year of my life. My vague, instinctive resistance to the coins as legal tender—as pure purchasing power—added to their worth. Somehow I knew that I would never spend them, never convert them into baseball cards or Slurpees or rides at the Evergreen State Fair. I didn't view them as vehicles for my desire; they were things in themselves, they held their own fascination, and I knew the continuing life of that fascination depended entirely on taking them out of circulation. As they lost currency, an element of worthlessness thus entered into my idea of money, an aesthetic dimension. I understood that their value increased the more they sank into the past, and because of this the coins had some of the quality of buried treasure. At that age, I lost things, I broke them or outgrew them, my interests changed, but I guarded those seven silver dollars jealously, aware of the link between their personal interest to me and their significance in the world. The coins had very little real toy value. I couldn't throw them or use them to improvise scenarios of valor or heroism; and I couldn't include anyone else in my play, as I did with my guns and Tonka trucks. I kept the coins in a leather purse that was shaped like a boot, a souvenir my father brought home from a trip to Tucson, where he had presented a paper at an academic conference; the boot zipped shut, and MEXICO was printed across the sole. I hid the purse in the bottom drawer of my dresser, stuffed beneath clothes I no longer wore, but then there was a moment in which I decided it was time to put the whole thing—the boot-shaped purse and silver dollars both—in the bank.

The only times I'd actually been inside the bank were in the company of my father, who, among other things, taught business finance. In back of the bank was the vault, the door a polished steel slab with a spoked wheel such as you would find at the helm of a ship, and inside the vault was my father's safe deposit box. He kept important papers in the box, insurance policies and a few stock certificates that must have had sentimental value, as either early or important trades he'd made in his career, because normally a man with my father's acumen would have held the issues in their street name. Also in the box, he kept an ornate silver watch and fob and penknife, a beautiful set stored in a case lined with crushed green velvet. It had belonged to his father, a man I'd never met. My father would set the watch on the table inside the vault and let me play with it while he shuffled through his papers, always telling me that his father had given it to him, and that he, in turn, would pass it on to me, when the time was right. Imagining that far-off juncture thrilled me, in large part because it implied that my father knew the future, and that he'd considered my place in it. I had only recently learned to tell time, and my sense of it was shaky, but I would pull the crown and adjust the delicate black hands until they closely matched those of the bank clock, then I would wind the stem and hold the watch to my ear, listening as the seconds ticked away inside.

My father seemed affable and relaxed in the bank, friendly with the tellers and the president alike. He addressed everyone by name, he flirted and joked, walked briskly and with confidence, taking command of the space. His own father had been a bookie and a figure of the Chicago underworld. More than once my father had seen him viciously beat other men over money, and I would come to understand, with time, that it had terrified my dad, seeing his father so violent in the conduct of business. As a young boy, he would visit the local precinct, first with my grandmother, then on his own, to bail his father out of jail. Because they were on the take, the police had to make a show of arresting my grandfather periodically, and on those occasions my father would come to the station, only to find his dad laughing and joking and playing cards with the cops who'd arrested him. My father's early education in money must have given him a glimpse of something savage and hollow in the heart of the system. The shock of that insight took the form of shame, as it does for so many of the sons of immigrants, and so now, as I look back, it makes perfect sense to me that my father's public self glowed in the company of people who did their business legitimately. His passion for securities—and common stock, particularly—was where he ultimately acquired his citizenship; in the bank, or on the phone with a broker, or in class teaching others about finance, he acted like a man with the rights and privileges of a native, a status his own father had never fully attained. Funny, charming, seemingly at ease— he became these things the minute he walked through the bank door. He especially loved the buildings that housed the institutions of money, banks among them. The enormous trust implied by the whole system was palpable to him, perhaps because he knew the fragility of it first hand, how beneath the flirtation and joking, the first names and handshakes, without some essential civil arrangement between people, it could always devolve into brutal beatings.

People who knew him in his capacity as a money-wiz have told me that he was a genius, and there's no question that he was a smart man. Whether he was explaining why cigarettes were price inelastic or describing the dissonant notion behind fairly standard ideas of diversification (that you're actually seeking an utter lack of correlation as a form of harmony), you felt the force and elegance of his mind—and at our house, this kind of stuff was table talk. And so what happened with my silver dollars and my shoe-purse is a mystery, a moment that I've returned to again and again over the years. The whole thing had the character of a lesson, of something more than a simple transaction. Put plainly, here is how I remember it. My father and I drove to the bank and stood in line and waited for a teller. When it was our turn, I reached up and stuck my shoe on the counter, which was about level with my chin. My father had instructed me at lunch that I would do all the talking, and we had even rehearsed the lines, so I said to the woman that I wanted to put my purse and silver dollars in the bank. Even to this day, I can see myself standing there, I know the hour, the weather outside as seen through the bank's high windows, the slight feeling of confusion, the hesitance as I wondered if my words were making sense, the coldness at my temples where a faint doubt registered. My father exchanged a glance with the teller, and I looked back, over my shoulder, at the vault, and when he asked me if I was sure, I said yes, because that was our script, that was the story we had rehearsed and agreed to tell. The teller did her work, and then handed me back my empty shoe and a green savings book. At this point I was so flustered that I couldn't summon the courage to tell her what I was thinking—that the shoe was part of it, that I wanted my leather boot in the bank too.

Naturally, when I went to retrieve the silver dollars they were gone; and yet I was devastated when I was handed, instead, seven ordinary dollar bills. I felt rooked. All the alchemy of imagination that had brought me to the bank, that had enlarged the idea of those silver dollars, was undone. What has remained curious to me over the years is why my father didn't see what was happening and intervene. He had all the savvy, while in some ways my idea of the bank was based on banks in old Westerns. For me, it was a place where people stored money, and where criminals could grab it, if clever or brutal enough. The bank kept money safe. It was the physical place, it was the vault with the polished steel door, it was the safe deposit box in which I'd store my silver dollars beside the watch and fob that would one day be mine, when the time was right. Most of all, the bank was where my father and

I spent some of our best days, the rare place where I saw him happy and at home, his private and increasingly troubled and violent self set aside in favor of the public man who was upright and worthy and could stride across the carpet to shake the president's hand. It seems so obvious now, but ultimately that's what I was investing in when I decided to put my silver dollars in the bank, that future with my father.

Our business at the bank finished, we took a walk. Town was only one block long but my father was dressed for Michigan Avenue, dapper in his wingtips, navy blue blazer, and the sort of rakish flat cap favored by southern Italians. I wore dungarees and leather boots and a green flannel shirt from Penney's. I kept a native's eye on the Sammamish, where sockeye ran in the fall, flashing red in the slow murk of the slough, and a disused granary that rumor said was full of rats, but to my father that beckoning world was terra incognita, and at the corner, already impatient, the main drag used up, he steered me across the street, leading us toward what we called our "secret destination." It was fun to play along with my father in this conspiracy, to hold this secret in common, though we'd both known all along exactly where the day would end. We were going to the bakery and we were going to eat chocolate cake.

On the way there my father mentioned that when he was a boy he had a favorite uncle who gave him a Morgan silver dollar every Christmas. He didn't need to explain to me that the seven Morgans I'd just put in the bank were the direct descendants of that distant gesture.

"Where's your uncle now?" I asked.

"I'm not sure," my father said. And then, in a way that registered very strangely for me, he added, "He was unmarried."

I didn't know what my father meant but I never forgot what he said. My ear seized on the distortion, heard the lurch in logic, the faltering fact: unmarried. He seemed to have answered a question I hadn't asked, drawing on a depth that was wholly private. Briefly, he was alone. In the worshipping eyes of a son any father's life is epic, I suppose, but nothing in my father's life ever approached the coherence of narrative. He was, I know, a proud and high-minded man, but with the kind of rigid pride and impossible rectitude that's a form of suppression, an immigrant son's pride, the triumphant pride, namely, of having overcome the past. In his epic life the trail of evidence was scant, the facts meager and few; an odd scattering of fragments and then a vast surrounding silence. That unmarried uncle was one such fragment, but my father would return to this uncle so often, feeding off the same thin fact, that I began to collect the pieces, storing them up as zealously as I had guarded my silver dollars. And so, in time, this one false note, this strange detail, this favorite uncle, this unmarried uncle eventually acquired a name, he was Chris, he was Uncle Chris, an Uncle Chris who lived alone, alone in a single room, a room that was spare and clean, a small cheap room in a flophouse on Chicago's near West Side, and one day, a winter day, my grandfather, Antonio D'Ambrosio, viciously beat his brother and left him, this brother, this Uncle Chris, the giver of silver dollars, bloody and unconscious in a hillock of dirty snow beneath the El tracks at Argyle.

The Argyle El stop served as my grandfather's front, and all through elementary school my father, always a go-getter, worked the counter in the afternoons and on weekends. In his mind the front was the family business, a Father & Son operation, and it was his job to hustle commuter sundries, all the newspapers, magazines, cigarettes and candy that would show sufficient income on my grandfather's modest but fraudulent tax returns. "I saw him beat the living daylights out of my Uncle Chris," my father would tell me, years later, in language that had never escaped 1944. "It was ugly," he said. "I ran," he said. "I ran the hell out of there, I ran all the way to the lake and"—with a dismissive wave of his hand he shut the story down, a thing beyond words, pointless to try, what can you say? He ran and it was winter and in his fear he'd fled without his coat. Now whenever I visit Chicago I make the same run myself, chasing after my father, pursuing him all the way down Argyle, crossing the Outer Drive until I too hit the lake. My father doesn't know I do this, and he probably wouldn't care or even understand, and really, I have no idea why this lunatic errand matters to me, beyond the foolish belief that, one of these days, when I reach the lake's edge, I will find him, I mean literally find him, still there, an eleven year old boy, cold and alone, with nowhere else to run.

Late at night my grandfather would crush saltine crackers in a coffee mug and fill it with cold milk. That was his favorite snack, and the sweetest memory my father ever shared with me. Whenever I imagine it I'm right there with him, looking over his shoulder in some half-lit, long-ago kitchen, watching a boy watch a man he loves spoon a gruel of milk and saltines into his mouth as he totes the vig on a loan or reads over the race results in the Chicago Tribune, tallying up the winners he'll pay off and the losers whose money he'll pocket. I have a somewhat desperate need to witness the scene and to know my father had that love, that small store of tenderness in his memory. My grandfather worked twelve hours a day, six days a week and then seven during World War II, when so many horses ran at Mexican tracks. He went to sleep at 2 AM, he woke at 8 AM. He rarely attended church but he tithed and then some, always the single largest contributor to St. Thomas of Canterbury's coffers, back in the days when those numbers were brazenly published in church bulletins. In a bookie's universe cash flows constantly, and then there's the siphoning. His front at the Argyle El stop was prime real estate and it's unlikely that the cops at the local precinct were the only people he greased. In that era, on the North Side of Chicago, he would have answered to Hymie Weiss, Bugs Moran and, later, Paul Ricca, heir to the Capone Syndicate.

I find it much harder to imagine the intricacies of my father's confusion as he walked to the precinct, suddenly the man of the house, an envelope of cash in his pocket. Once he had the drill down, once he realized he wouldn't find his father behind bars, in prison stripes, guarded by men with drawn guns, it only took him ten minutes to make his dad's bail. The sham arrests kept the record straight, but the hero of the story was cash. Cash was magic, cash was powerful, cash was the savior. Although I imagine the short walk home was conducted in silence—after all, this was just another day on the job—I suspect that in some tacit but troubled agreement an economist was busy being born. I can guess what my father would say now, belatedly filling the silence, and here's my weak imitation of his mind at work: to legitimize an illegal business such as bookmaking, you needed the approbation of the law, or at least the approval of the people who enforce the law. Those enforcers grant the bookmaker a license that isn't legally theirs to give, but which, by virtue of their position, they have the power to create or destroy at whim. The law enforcers charge a fee for the mythical but economically significant license and, to protect both themselves and the licensee, they create an insurance policy, issued to the bookie, that provides ongoing protection for the life of the illegal business. Neither the insurance and its protections nor the license are free. There is a cost to everything. There are no free lunches.

Of course, graft and corruption and gambling make a grab at the free lunch and the D'Ambrosios did more than OK in America. They owned their six-flat outright, my father was enrolled in a fine Jesuit academy and was meeting Catholic "swells" from all around the city, and he had at his disposal a new black Buick with a necker's knob on the steering wheel, which allowed him to coolly turn a corner and squeeze a date's thigh at the same time. Then in 1950, Antonio D'Ambrosio dropped dead of a heart attack on the sidewalk outside his Argyle front. He was fifty-two years old. In the box on his death certificate for USUAL OCCUPATION my grandfather was listed as "Proprietor" and in the box for KIND OF BUSINESS a clerk neatly printed "Cigar Store." He passed away a month after my father finished high school. I know nothing about those days except that my father had the key to a safe deposit box, and at the bank, when he was alone in the vault, in the quiet of the armored walls, with the day gate locked, he turned the key, opened the box, and found one hundred thousand dollars, cash. Or, in today's dollars, my father turned that key and opened the lid on a million dollars. That, as my father would say, is a nice chunk of change.

My father didn't want the burden, particularly the burden of his mother, my grandmother, who beat him pitilessly with a broom handle all through his boyhood. "The broom treatment," he called it, without any elaboration. It's not hard for me to imagine that those beatings did all the things beatings do to people. Still, the moment he turned the key and opened that safe deposit box his career in finance was determined, and my grandmother would live off the money, conservatively managed by her son, for the next thirty-six years. The bookie's boy went legit, breaking with his father, and yet, a good son, kept his hand in a world whose fated, narcotic action is gambling's kissing cousin. Instead of handicapping horses he played the market, trading racing sheets for Value Line, and his career in finance was, in some ways, an apologia for a life of crime. That early death broke my father, dividing him from his past, but the heavy tectonics of one of our most cherished myths—that each new generation will surpass the previous—did a lot of the heaving and sundering too. It's a brutal business, making Americans. As soon as he finished his dissertation, looking for a fresh start, my father found a job in a world as remote from Chicago as he could imagine, in a place neither he nor anyone in his family could really picture, and was carried along on the buoyant currents of yet another American myth, moving as far west as he could go and still be standing on the continental US.

Which brings us to the secret destination. Warm from the sun, warm from the ovens, warm from the smell of rising yeast and freshly baked bread, all this safe and sleepy warmth was a kind of quiet, and in that white-tiled Dutch bakery my father's voice, I remember, boomed a little too loudly, waking the place to life. He tapped the counter bell twice and when a stout woman with her hair in a snood appeared my father was already reaching deep into his pocket. As sophisticated as he was about every manner of financial instrument, cash was where it was at, cash was holy, and all his life my father kept bricks of it, bill-strapped at the bank, stored in a safe at home. His stash, he called it. He always had to have his stash. And whenever he plunged a hand into his left pocket it was time for ostentation. He'd stretch his arms out to clear his cuffs, hold his gaudy gold money clip chest high, lick his fingers and flick through bills, a c-note on the outside, of course, implying wealth in a fat wad that might in fact hide a poor truth, that the bulk of the bankroll was made up of singles, then he'd snap off one, two, three bills, whatever was needed. This wasn't the father with the doctoral dissertation on railroad economics. This was someone else, this was my father in his fluency, flashing his cash and slapping a sawbuck on the counter as if we were back in Chicago, maybe the Empire Room at the Palmer House, and not a bakery in the boonies on a Saturday afternoon. I watched the whole performance from a tiny table by the window. We'd done our business at the bank and now we each had big piece of chocolate layer cake, thick with icing. It was yellow cake. I don't know how they got it yellow but they did and the yellow was beautiful against the warm brown frosting. We loved that chocolate cake. This was a good day, a really good day, and I knew what was coming next. My father stared for a long while out the window, at what, I don't know, but I waited, waited for his famous phrase, sure it would come, and when his reverie broke and he returned to the bakery and our little table, he smiled at me, then looked down at his cake, and there it was, sure as rain.

"This is living," he said, "huh, Charlie boy?"

Of course, of course—the past followed him out west, and now we had our own history, easily as troubled as the one he'd left behind in Chicago and far more violent. Every time I visited my father I was certain it would be the last. Months would go by, even a year, and I wouldn't know whether he was dead or alive, and then I would see a sign—a leaf falling just so, a plastic sack blowing through an empty intersection— and corny as those omens were, the spookiness was real to me, always there, lurking below the surface of my days, and would haunt and harass me until the only cure was to call him again. Or I'd pay him a visit after dwelling on some silly, old, odd, obscure chain of memory. Other times I'd show up intending business, bringing a family grievance to the table. He'd sent my sister a letter smeared with his blood. He'd tried to sell his mentally-ill son a cemetery plot. He'd shown up at several of my readings wearing a Chicago Cubs hat dangling with fishing lures, a crown of thorns fashioned from spinners and spoons and treble-hooked crankbaits, and then he'd just stand there, thirty feet away, staring and saying nothing while I signed books, in a grotesque martyrdom that I somehow understood.

One day I was drinking coffee on a bench in Victor Steinbrueck Park, at the north end of the Public Market, next to a Japanese man, who was reading what I believed to be a biography of Hitler. The title was *Hitler*, anyway. His son sat between us, a little boy of roughly four; he was bored and antsy, pestering his father with questions that went unanswered. "What year did you first exist in, Daddy? When did you first come alive?" In his frustration the boy kept trying to close the book, slapping at it and mussing the pages, and the father kept pushing him away. I finished my coffee and walked to the south end of the Market and called my father from a payphone outside Delaurenti's, an Italian grocery, asking if he'd eaten. He hadn't. I brought spaghetti and meatballs, buffalo mozzarella and roasted peppers, green olives stuffed with pimentos, and a jar of hot pepperoncini, indulgences out of his past, hoping the feast might provoke that old famous phrase, but the food didn't matter. Nothing in this world seemed to matter anymore. Instead he kept referring to the mystics, as if in fact those mystics were in the room. "As the mystics tell us," he would say, "all is well, all is well." In rejecting the material world, he seemed to have found an alibi, an elsewhere, glorying in a triumph that was hard for me to hear. He would eventually make himself destitute, giving all his money, every scrimped nickel, to the Catholic Church, becoming a ward of the dioceses. This *contemptus mundi* included his kids; he wanted it known that he did not need us for his happiness, did not need us at all. He no longer spoke to any of his seven children. He rarely left his apartment. He was a physical mess, obese, wheezing, unable to lift himself from his chair without tremendous exertion. Now and then I could see the old fire in my father's eyes, and with the urgency of some thought roiling inside him he would struggle forward, but he seemed trapped in his body, wholly bound by his physical decline. The great and engaging brilliance, and the passion that made it so infectious and forceful, was struggling, it seemed, toward an apophatic mysticism, negating facts and fictions and emptying itself of pride and all its projects. He was done with all those corrupt and violent appetites, but alone, divested of business and free of family, the unknowing was agonized. After we'd eaten, as I washed and dried the dishes and a hard rain whipped against the windows, my father said, "You know, I've never been to the rainforest. Isn't that a hell of a thing?" It seemed terrible to have come so close to the ocean and never set foot in the Pacific, as if his journey west were never completed, but when I offered to drive him out to the coast he waved me off.

"As the Desert Fathers tell us," he said, "all is well, all is well."

At the end of the night he led me down the hall to a closet and gave me what remained of a box of red pens and asked if I wanted his old safe. It was beige, about the size of a milk crate, and weighed at least 100 pounds. I took it, I said yes, just because he'd spent the night renouncing the world, trying to let go, and I felt that I might offend his pride by refusing this parting gift. I carried the safe down the corridor and sat on it, breathing hard, while I waited for the elevator. It was one of those nights in Seattle when the wind downtown was strong enough to blow flowerpots off the decks of high rises and the traffic signals danced a crazed tarantella over the empty intersections. The streets down there were always drifting with deranged characters but that night even people with nowhere to go had found somewhere to go. The weight of the safe was ponderous and uncooperative, too heavy to hoist on my shoulder for long, impossibly awkward to carry in front of me. The die-cast edges cut my fingers, and it took me forever to lurch and waddle the five blocks home. Every fifty feet or so I dropped the safe on the sidewalk, gasping for breath. Then I'd sit on it and roll a cigarette, smoking in the rain. I wondered if passing cops would think I was a thief, in an inept heist, making an even more pathetic getaway. I wish I could say that I did the sensible thing, ditching the safe in a dumpster or abandoning it on someone's stoop, but I didn't, I carried it as far as I possibly could. By the time I got back to my apartment I was too wet and miserable and exhausted to haul the safe up the stairs, and I had no use for it anyway. I didn't have the combination and I didn't own anything valuable. I left the safe in the alley behind my building, in a patch of dirt beneath a tall cedar, and it stayed there for a long time. No one took it because it was heavy and it was empty. And then one morning I looked out my window and it was gone. ❖

Documents

Poem by father (1972)

One Sunday morning when I was a boy, my father came out of his office and handed me a poem. It was about a honeybee counseling a flea to flee a doggy and see the sea. The barbiturates my father took to regulate his emotions made him insomniac, and I understood that he'd been awake most of the night, laboring over these lines, listing all the words he could think of ending in a long *e*. This meant using many adverbs and the elevated *thee* as a form of address. My father was a professor of finance who wrote fairly dry textbooks, where the prose marched in soldierly fashion across the page, broken by intricate formulas calculating risk and return, and this poem was a somewhat frilly production for him. The poem was an allegory about his desire to leave our family. Like a lot of people my father felt a poem was a bunch of words with a tricky meaning deeply buried away, like treasure, below a surface of rhyming sounds. I was twelve years old, and I understood the sense of the poem instantly, but the strange mixture of childish diction and obvious content silenced me. I was ashamed. That Sunday morning I was sitting on the living room floor, on a tundra of white carpet my father considered elegant. The drapes were closed, because he worried that the sun would fade the fabric on the furniture, but a bright bar of light cut through a gap in the curtains, and that's where I sat, since it was warm there, in a house where we were otherwise forbidden to adjust the thermostat above sixty-two degrees.

Letter from younger brother (1997)

Not long ago, I was in Seattle, sitting in a café downtown. It was raining. I'd been there for some time before I realized that someone was staring at me through the window. I turned around and saw worn tennis shoes and dirty gray sweats. The man outside the window was my brother Mike. My father had three sons.

I'm the eldest; Danny, the youngest, killed himself sixteen years ago.

In addition to the tennis shoes and sweats, Mike was wearing a white T-shirt that hung to his knees and a black leather jacket he'd bought with VA money at a thrift store. His thinning hair was soaked, and his face had the pallor of warm cheese. In a plastic sack he carried a carton of cigarettes he'd bought at the Navy PX. He's schizophrenic, and on some level I'm always aware that he's a stranger. I went outside and we talked and, in talking, we were brothers again. He did not look good; he was shivering. He was several miles from his halfway house, but when I offered to give him a ride he said, quite happily, that he preferred to walk. He started up the hill, limping a little from a pelvic injury he received, years ago, when he tried to kill himself by jumping off the Aurora Bridge in Seattle. Very soon he was gone.

Only a few years ago, Mike had been doing much better, and he wrote letters regularly, often two or three a month. Here is one:

Dear Char,

Mike here, who is there? I am fine as a blade of grass. How about you?

As I was leaving church the other day there was an opportunity to be part of a poor person's Kriss Kringle. I decided to buy an AIDS patient some high-quality gloves. The situation reminded me of Danny—I don't know why. The gift will be given to him although I believe I will never actually see the recipient. I will give him a card that says, "To a friend I don't know."

I don't think of Danny a lot. I don't feel pain about his death a lot either. Jesus has stepped into his boots and has replaced him. It caused me to heal and be born again. It is really quite beautiful. My heart is still with that kid like you cannot believe—or I suppose you could. Love can play a trick on you. It can cause you pain like you were suffering in hell but it is still love and still beautiful like heaven and the heaven and the hell of it are woven into one fabric, which is love. It's a mindblower to think like that but that is what Danny has done to me.

Call or write please.

I don't own a cat or dog—but I do the same by looking at squirrels and crows. I plan to buy some peanuts to feed the squirrels and bread for the birds. It is so much cheaper and I enjoy it the same as having my own animal.

When I pray I can see my life flash before my eyes. It is very beautiful. My life flashes before my eyes about twenty times a year. Other stuff like that happens to me also.

I've been through so much since becoming mentally ill—most of it, believe it or not, was good. Because of that I became sort of an indestructible man.

Love, Mike

Letter from youngest brother (November 26, 1986)

My brother Danny wrote his suicide note in my bedroom, and then, after a caesura that I know exists because he had to put down the pen in order to pick up the gun, he shot himself. For some reason, I've always been concerned about the length of the lapse, whether he reread what he'd written or stared dumbly at his signature, his name the final piece in a puzzling life he was about to end, before he pressed the gun to his head and pulled the trigger. Most suicides go about the last phase of their business in silence and don't leave notes. Death itself is the summary statement, and they step into its embrace hours or days before the barrel is finally raised to the roof of the mouth or the fingertips last feel the rough metal of the bridge rail. They are dead and then they die. But Danny wrote a note, or not so much a note as an essay, a long document full of self-hatred and sorrow, love and despair, and now I'm glad that I have it, because, this way, we're still engaged in a dialogue. His words are there and so is his hand, a hand I'd held, but, more important, one that left words, like an artifact, that are as real and physical to me as the boy who, at twenty-one, in a November long ago, wrote them.

I read the pages he wrote two or three times a month, often enough so that the words ring like the lines of poems I know well. All the struggle is still there in the headlong sentences that tumble toward his signature, in the misspelled words and syntactical errors, in the self-conscious language of a boy starved for love and trying, instead, to live a moment more off pride. The note has the back-and-forth of a debate, of words equally weighed and in balance, of a slightly agonized civility. He says, "I stopped making dreams." He says, "I don't know why I am doing this. I don't want to. I have dreams." He says that there is no God and that God is looking over his shoulder as he writes, making editorial remarks. He says, "I am glorifying myself now. I am afraid to stop writing though. I want to keep talking." He says, "I don't know what to say except I am sorry and I love. I love the whole family quite a bit and the terrible—" He clearly wants to find a way back, but he can't. He asks that we keep "the way" he died a secret and, as though he were done, signs his name. But on the next page, the last, he again asks that we keep "the way" he died secret, and again he signs his name. Much of the note is printed and those letters stand upright, but in the end Danny slips permanently into a sloping cursive as despair and self-hatred accelerate beyond return, as if he were being pulled down by the dark undercurrent of his life, his last words looping quickly across the page, continuous as breath.

Letter from eldest brother (2001)

Two years ago, I moved to Philipsburg, Montana. In the fall, I went for walks and brought home bones. The best bones weren't on trails—deer and moose don't die conveniently—and soon I was wandering so far into the woods that I needed a map and compass to find my way home. When winter came and snow blew into the mountains, burying the bones, I continued to spend my days and often my nights in the woods. I vaguely understood that I was doing this because I could no longer think; I found relief in walking up hills. When the night temperatures dropped below zero, I felt visited by necessity, a baseline purpose, and I walked for miles, my only objective to remain upright, keep moving, preserve warmth. When I was lost, I told myself stories, recounting my survival, implying that I would live and be able to look back at it all. At some point, I realized that I was telling my father these stories.

I decided that I would try corresponding with him. I had built a lean-to at seven thousand feet, and I routinely slept there. In the morning, I warmed myself by a fire and then walked home and began writing. I worked for days, even weeks, on the letters. The last time I'd seen him he made a point of showing me the stains in his bed, on the sheets. He pulled away the blankets, revealing bright yellow splotches of mustard, red patches of spaghetti sauce, something urinous that had spilled from a carton of take-out Chinese. I'm not sure what he meant to show me, and I'm not sure what saddened me more, this man eating alone in bed, who could not clean up after himself, or this man who needed to share with his son a grotesque failure.

My father and I had survived the same wounds. His lost sons were my brothers. I believed we might have something to talk about. I was drawn to the antique idea of a correspondence because it seemed restrained and formal, even ritualized. In Philipsburg, there is no home delivery, and people go to town to pick up mail. I always walked to the post office with my dog, and even that little effort, the mile of dirt road, blowing with dust or drifting with snow, made the mail that much more meaningful.

I delayed sending my first letter for several months. My father replied with a long, bulleted outline. I read it, bullet by bullet, feeling disoriented, despite the orderly indents and the nesting of what, in outlines, are called "children." After four or five readings I was able to breathe normally. I reread his outline until I lost its meaning, then got out my colored pens and began highlighting. The bullets and dashes and indentations were like the sleeves and straps and buckles of a straitjacket. I've often thought that the unit of measure that best suits prose is the human breath, but there was no air in my father's sentences; he seemed to be suffocating inside them.

I had made an effort to discuss the events of our past, but he regarded this as a trespass. "When did God empower you," he asked me, "with such omniscient abilities?" His position was truth; mine was not. My letter, he wrote, "is incorrect throughout, is a fictional ('Having no foundation in fact,' *OED*) version of reality ('Reality: The quality of being real or having an actual existence,' *OED*)." He was defensive, which I should have anticipated: "After nine years of sixty-hour weeks of intensive research, not reading and study, but research, I know I was a terrific dad and terrific husband."

I wrote more letters. His replies were long—seven, eight, nine pages. There were words he couldn't get past. He became obsessed with *boundaries*. Boundaries were bad. "Those who set them up," he wrote, "protect the dysfunctionality they see in themselves and seek to foist that malady on others through their boundaries." Boundaries, he wrote, "are the antithesis of meaningful honest relations." Boundaries have no place between a father and his children. He insisted the proper word was *relation*. "Relation is a mathematical notion which means one-to-one correspondence."

Another time it was the word *gag*. He had used the word, saying that I was prevented from speaking honestly; I objected; he objected to my objection. "Emphasis on the word, *gag*, denies the act!!! The gag is the aggressive act. The word *gag* fits, is proportional to, the act. The gag is the loaded act; the word *gag* fits the denigrative power of the act. The act, not the word, is aggressive and odious. Place the focus where it belongs, properly, on the aggressive and repugnant act, and not on the word."

Some nights, I dug into the lee of a snowdrift and hollowed a shelter for myself. Snow contains air and insulates, holding the body's warmth so that, at a certain point, the temperature remains constant, blood and ice in equilibrium. In deep snow, I dragged supplies with a pulk I'd made from a child's sled and plastic conduit. I was afraid of avalanches and checked a slope meter before traversing open, treeless hillsides. What I feared was suffocation, particularly the inability to make my chest expand. I really knew nothing about winter, nothing about surviving the season beyond the blunt lesson in fatality I'd learned from picking up bones. Sometimes I slept in the open mouths of mine shafts, their crumbled headframes like broken teeth, where twice I found clusters of bats, hanging by their feet, their wings folded in, like the strange fruits of darkness itself.

I wrote, asking him about our home movies. For years I'd kept alive the fantasy that he burned the movies, only because I was haunted by the image of them orphaned in a Salvation Army thrift shop, reels and reels of birthdays, Christmases, and Easters, all reduced to an ironic treasure for strangers. In the past, I had wanted to believe my father was a liar rather than a man who could destroy something so valuable to his children. The movies were old Super 8s, poorly lit and without sound, but the only place left where I could see my brother's face.

I wrote, "You intentionally destroyed something inside your children, a place of warmth and fondness, a cherished dream, a continuity that connects us in time to our history and across space to one another."

His response was icy: "Of what sense of warmth and fondness are you speaking? It is an interesting sentiment, laced with some romanticism, but devoid of reality." And he wanted to know, "What did I destroy in you that was not already destroyed?"

In my father's last letter, the grammar carries the summary tone of a narrative closing down. It is framed by the forms of family affection. He opens with "Dear Char" and parts with "Love," followed by his signature. In between, the language suggests closure, termination. My previous letter, he says, continued an "unacceptable tenor and dead-end focus." It smacked of "recidivism"; it followed a "desolate and vacuous path." None of my letters "added a repairment." "So be it," he says.

I sometimes wonder if by "repairment" he meant "repayment," and I always pause at the caesura created by the simple sentence, "So be it," which Catholic kids were once taught is the meaning of "Amen." Was this the phrase that ran through my brother's mind as he paused between his two signatures? *So be it*: with these, my father's last words, I know I will never hear from him again. But I save his letters, as I save Danny's, as I save Mike's, neatly bound and held between the army surplus boots that my brother died in, and which I keep, filled with rocks, on my desk. ❖

PART 2:
STRATEGIES
AGAINST EXTINCTION

Above all, the real is arbitrary. For to be a realist (in art or in life) is to acknowledge that all things might be other than they are. That there is no design, no intention, no aesthetic or moral or teleological imprimatur but, rather, the equivalent of Darwin's great vision of a blind, purposeless, ceaseless evolutionary process that yields no "products"—only temporary strategies against extinction.

—JOYCE CAROL OATES, "They All Just Went Away"

American Newness

Right inside the door of my first Fleetwood Home I was greeted by the evocative odor of American Newness, that smell everyone knows but cannot name. It was like breaking the seal on a box and getting a whiff of—of what?—of exactly what you always wanted. I know I got doped up on the smell and instantly forgot the facts of my life for the fantasy it might become. The walls in the homes I toured had the texture of those egg-shaped confections of sugar that house dioramic Easter scenes of bunnies and baby chickens. The walls didn't look entirely dry, as though you might sink your finger in for a lick of buttercream frosting. They were immaculate and white and somehow against this backdrop even normal objects seemed like miniatures, not quite real and thus easily manageable. All the rooms were furnished by a hired decorator but felt empty. What they were missing was you and yet it was haunting to confront a face in a mirror. Suddenly you were there, arrived and occupying a place in this world premised on choice, where everything exists as potential, where the deep pile carpet on the floor is only a polite suggestion and might, in a moment's wish, become Adobe, Cameo Blush, Cabernet, Cinnabar, Periwinkle, or Nappa [sic] Valley. The Formica on the counter could be traded for squares of blue tile. The fridge will find food, the quiet will find voices, the beds will bring rest and love and renewal.

To make a manufactured home, first you build a chassis with axles. After you've put the chassis in place you glue and staple the flooring to it with extra-big boards that cut down on the number of seams and hence reduce the likelihood of leakage. As it's being built the house floats like a river barge on a bed of compressed air. A couple men lean into it with their shoulders and shove it from one station to the next as if it were nothing. Exterior walls go up, interior walls; men plumb the thing, run wires, install fixtures; they add windows, hang doors; a roof is lowered in place by an Erector Set crane; appliances, cabinets, fans, and carpets are readied. Out of this wizardly and truly awesome Oz the house is wheeled into the daylight and trucked away to whatever Kansas your heart desires.

I made a couple of trips to the factory and a dirt lot nearby where Fleetwood showcases their finished product, and lastly I started looking for places where I could find people living in the houses for real. Several detours off Interstate 5 showed me just how rapidly a community seeded with modular housing can grow. Everything's so brand-new there isn't even any sound in the air. In one such neighborhood off Gun Club Road in Woodland, Washington, I parked my truck and tried to talk to some kids coming home from school, but they were right on it with the snappy, drilled response.

"Are you a stranger?" one little girl wanted to know.

"What's a stranger?"

"Somebody who kills you or rapes you," she said.

I'm not that kind of stranger, but it might have been here, in this neighborhood, in this place where the children know what to say, that a note of sorrow first entered the world of hope I'd been entertaining during my initial home tour.

Your typical manufactured home makes its way in the world because it bears a studied resemblance to a regular house. Its visual ambition is mimetic and realistic the same way a painting of a cow agreeably satisfies verisimilitude if it's got four legs, a tail, and a head. You could build these homes attractively but the aesthetic would need to be stripped and lean and frank, with materials that openly declare themselves and hide nothing. Fleetwood, by contrast, makes a sincere imitation of the real thing, a house that aspires to popularity and recognition like a girl who comes to the prom with a face on loan from a magazine. It's that inserted layer of sincerity that rings false. It's evilly un-American to say aloud, but real divisions exist between people, and the houses themselves try hard, desperately hard, to obscure those differences. They're socially insecure yet hopeful. They want acceptance and to get it they try really hard to please everyone.

The woman who gave me my factory tour was so sweet, so kind, so eager to encourage my optimistic assessment of Fleetwood's product, the echo of everything she said now rattles around in my head because I knew before I entered the building I'd betray her trust and hope. She told me she herself lived in a Fleetwood triple-wide and was absolutely happy. Like everyone connected with Fleetwood she was defensive against unspoken snottiness, and given my inability to rise above it I can see why. "I hope you say something nice," nice people kept saying to me in person and on the phone.

Salespeople and secretaries alike insisted that a Fleetwood Home was every bit the structural and social equal of what's known in the trade as a stick-built house. Their zeal was evangelistic, it was memorized and rehearsed and recited like a prayer, it was felt and sincere and thus a notch shy of being spontaneously true. What people were telling me was no more a syncretic hodgepodge than the Pledge of Allegiance, but if you don't live entirely within it, if you're not unself-consciously at home in the words and you hesitate even a little, it all starts to sound like cant.

In the face of so much generous and heartfelt uplift I cut short the factory tour, asking no questions. This woman and all these people, they are the good people, whereas I was just walking around in the factory faking my enthusiasm and hiding a creepy low-grade horror. Normally I don't like my meaning ready-made, but by the time I headed out to my truck I was in total despair about not being with the program.

I drove up along the Lewis River for a change of scene and to think and to see if anybody was catching fish from an early fall run of chinook. A GOOD ATTITUDE IS A TREASURE, said the sign outside the Woodland Middle School, on my way upriver. Five miles back in the canyon the banks were crowded with fishermen working fairly dull, obvious water, where the highly evolved homing instinct of the salmon hits the blunt obstruction of a dam and the fish pool up in mass confusion. At the hatchery there was the usual display of agitprop about salmon recovery and an article about the building of the first dam and how it might just possibly disrupt and ruin the runs. It did, of course, and now the Lewis is only the ghost of itself, flowing emptily into the Columbia. The article was written in 1930 and seventy years later the river no longer seriously produces salmon but continues to spin the turbines that supply power to the recessed lights in the kitchens of modular homes up and down I-5. An abiding American assumption, mentally apocalyptic, says that somehow the wrongs in history stem from our ignorance; once we're enlightened, we'll be free of our errant ways and history itself will stop and we'll come to rest in a return to Eden. Now the state of Washington raises fish in rearing ponds and releases smolts into the river, hoping their intricate salmonoid nerves won't give out in complete bafflement and, after four years at sea, they'll find their way back upriver to the cul-de-sac of their birth.

It wasn't my original plan but I checked into a motel for the night because it bugged me that I couldn't find anything nice to say about modular homes. I ate dinner at a Mexican restaurant across the street. It was karaoke night in a lounge the hostess referred to as "the cantina." The décor was modular Mexican, a sort of mañana peon style that lightly revamped clichés about lazy Mexicans. Two guys at my table told me they were hiding from their wives, they'd kind of karaoked a lie about working on their cars and instead came to the cantina for a couple quick rum and Cokes. Another guy's girlfriend was out of town and he kept asking me what I thought of the waitress's ass. He was embarrassing me and I felt square and stupid and unable to say what, as a man, I know I'm supposed to say, and so, nervously changing the subject, I asked him about the fishing on the Lewis. He said, "Look, we took the land from the Indians, like what? I don't know. Five hundred years ago? Was it five hundred years? Big deal. I'm all for paying them back, but after a generation or two, they should get in society like everyone else." Later I shared a table with a woman whose home business was writing personal poetry "for your weddings and funerals." She often writes letters for friends who need special thoughts expressed and many people have told her she should write a novel. Her husband recently convinced her to leave Portland and move to Woodland and then he left her for the woman next door and moved back to Portland. Divorce and treachery and betrayal were in the air but so was desire and the people who came forward to sing surprised me with their earnestness. I'd have thought this kind of thing a joke, snide and ironic, but they sang their hearts out. The favored narrative of the songs people selected turned on love and heartbreak and while the music and the words were not the singer's own, the voice and the feeling were. Emotion was evident by the way people gripped the microphone and bowed their heads as they waited eight bars for the chorus to come around and when it did they lifted their heads again and sang the words and moved toward the crowd compelled by an inner urgency.

My last day I still didn't feel like going home. I lingered, pointlessly. Overnight a banner had been strung across Woodland's main drag announcing the coming of "Make a Difference Day." I stopped a couple of places to look through a few more completed houses. All along I'd been intrigued by the lack of language inside these model homes. There were no words, spoken or written, and even the few decorative books seemed mute on the shelves—not words, but things. Language in the modular industry belongs largely to the manufacturing end of the business, and there, in technical brochures and spec sheets, it's thick and arcane, made up of portmanteaus and other odd hybrids that are practically Linnaean in their specificity. You get Congoleum and Hardipanel Siding and Nicrome Elements.

At the factory all that language is assembled and given narrative development in the tightly plotted path the house takes as it progresses from chassis to truck. But once inside the finished home it ends, there's a kind of white hush, a held breath, and all narrative, defined simply as a sequence of events in time, is gone. Silence and timelessness take over so that when the door opens and you cross the threshold you feel you've stepped out of life itself.

In house #19 I find an icy aspect to the arrangement of family artifacts and like Keats before the Grecian Urn I can't quite puzzle out the story. Photos have been framed and set out on tables and shelves but the pictures are of those same corny people who haven't aged a bit since they came with your first cheap wallet. Who are these blonde women with unfading smiles? Whose bright kids are these? What happy family is this? In the kitchen two ice cream sundaes sit on the counter. Those sundaes will never melt, nor will they be eaten. The cookbook in the kitchen is open to a recipe for blueberry pancakes but in the living room a bottle of wine and two glasses wait on a coffee table. What time of day is it?

In house #17 I encounter the only joke on the lot: EAT MORE PORK is stenciled on the side of a wooden chicken.

In house #12 it's Christmas.

In house #16 you've got a pastoral leitmotif in the prints on the walls and the folksy bric-a-brac on the shelves. I linger longest here. Outside I hear real church bells ring, dull and somewhat muffled through the dense (R-41) insulation. It's as though the bell is being clapped with a cotton tongue. Through the window I see a wedding party. I feel like a voyeur watching the bride and groom, inverting the business of a Peeping Tom. I have to sneak up on regular life. As much as rote irony informs my take on this, I've been imagining living in these homes, where I'd plunk one down, etc. What would I be able to see out my front window? A wedding! In the master bedroom down the hall the unwrinkled bed is empty, clean, without misery or past. Happy love has no history and this bed is its home. I'd like to come back some night and fuck in one of these modular houses. The perfection is inviting but really I just want to soil the sheets. I want to bring exhaustion into the equation. All these houses are waiting for the future to come and haunt them.

I've overstayed. On my way out I stop in the kitchen. A plastic dinner is set on the counter. Tonight and every night in this home where time has stopped and there's no story or words we're having fake turkey, we're having fake carrots too, fake carrots and asparagus and baked potatoes with sour cream and chives, and afterward, after this *tableau vivant* of bounty is cleared away, we'll grind coffee by hand in the wooden mill on the counter and serve it in the living room by the basket of logs for which, in #16 at least, there is no hearth.

Our boy will fall asleep on the rug and eventually I'll lift and carry him sleepily to the pine-log bed in his room, and after his prayers I'll tuck the quilt around his chin and tell him I love him.

Our girl will go to her room too, say her prayers too, beneath a picture of a roan horse, but in this case I'll only look on, from the doorway, as you bend to kiss her cheek.

Then you and I will go down the hall to sleep in that bed where no one's ever been before. ❖

Winning

Now what remains of the place is an anonymous wall of brick, but not so long ago my uncle ran a bar at 112 1/2 Clinton Street, the half being our family's share in the City of Big Shoulders, Chicago. If the Sears Tower were considered the gnomon of a sundial and you were inclined to tell time by organizing shadows, then the bar was located at roughly ten o'clock in the morning. By midmorning the shadows swept in, the air darkened and the streets turned silty, creating sunken rivers of early night, murky and unpromising to most people but suiting just fine the shady temper of the hardcore drinkers and gamblers the bar catered to. In fact they came precisely for that halfness, that demimonde aspect of the address. The building itself occupied an alley that had formerly served as a cattle run from the trains to the stockyards and packing plants on the South Side. Soon after the butchering ended the bar opened for business. It must have been a big improvement not to taste blood in the wind, blown over the city from the slaughter-houses. When I lived in Chicago those old abattoirs, long ago lost to history, had become inviolate and fixed in legend, but the city was changing again.

It was destroying itself, or sloughing off its old indus-trial self, and many of the brick warehouses and factory buildings in the neighborhood, gutted and window-less, deserted, were no better than caves hollowed from rock, with doors gaping open blackly, home to the homeless, the vast vacant interiors lit only by the light of fires burning in oil drums. In seeking the future a city like Chicago wrecks itself and returns to stone, at least briefly. There were piles of rubble such as you imagine in war, but the absence of declared enemies, and the lethargic unfolding of time, its leisurely pace, kept people from seeing the scale of the shift as cata-strophic. Factories and warehouses and hotels, these old muscular hopes came down in heaps of brick and mortar, of pulverized concrete and cracked limestone, and then those cairns of rock, in turn, were cleared off to become barren lots as flat and featureless as the prairie they'd supplanted. Now brand-new buildings staunchly occupy those spaces, but for the duration, for the brief winter, spring, and summer I lived and worked next door to the bar, there was the constant gray taste of mortar on my tongue, my lips burning from the lime it was laced with, as clouds of dust were set adrift by each new day's demolition.

Brick is relocated earth, and the streets of a city like Chicago re-create a riverbank, in this case the clay banks of both the Mississippi and Ohio Rivers, where a good portion of Chicago's brick originally came from. The mining of clay is often referred to as "winning," a curious kind of victory, considering the clay used in brickmaking comes from the Carboniferous period, a subcategory of the Paleozoic, some 340 million years ago. Such a vast span of time would seem to temper any man's sense of triumph. It was during the Carboniferous that amniote eggs allowed ancestral birds and reptiles to reproduce on land; flight was first achieved, too, as insects evolved wings. And then something happened, something happened to the birds and mammals and reptiles, to the nascent flying insects, to the whole ambition and direction of that geologic age. Everything died off and disappeared in that silent way only an eon can absorb and keep secret.

And yet with death the seedless vascular plants that existed in tropical swamp forests provided the organic material that became coal. These dead plants didn't completely decay but instead turned to peat bogs. When the sea covered the swamps, marine sediment covered the peat, and eventually intense pressure and heat transformed these organic remains into coal and shale. Curiously, burning brick in kilns only extends and completes the process epochal time itself used to form the source clay. Brick manufacturers use coal to fire and harden the clay, removing moisture and the last memory, the last vestiges of fluidity from the brick. (In fact there's a taxonomy of bricks based on how burnt they are: clinker brick, nearest the fire, becomes vitrified, glassy and brittle; red brick is the hardest and most desirable product of the kiln; and salmon brick, sitting farthest from the fire, is underburned and soft, unsuitable for exposed surfaces.) The obvious advantage of brick as a building material is that it's already burned, which accounts for its presence in Chicago after the fire of 1871. Brick transformed the city, ushering in an era of industrial greatness, completing—no, not completing, but extending—extending a process that began with a mysterious extinction, a vast unimagined loss.

During my time in Chicago my day job was to load cars and trucks with reproduction furniture, the historical imperative of which had vanished, vaguely, around the turn of the century. Nonetheless shoppers from the suburbs drove to the city to browse the warehouse, its four floors and forty thousand square feet of fake antiques. They bought oxblood leather wingbacks, banker's lamps, baker's racks, oak iceboxes, old phones with a crank on the side that would, with a turn or two, summon the operator. The furniture was hokey, farmy, Depressiony. Of course none of the people who shopped the warehouse were cutting blocks of winter ice to haul by horse and wagon and then pack and preserve in layers of straw for the long hot summer. They lived in the suburbs, they had appliances. It was curious and teleologically baffling. Why buy a phone you have to crank by hand when you can punch buttons to place your call? Why a wrought-iron baker's rack for men and women whose cookies and bread did their cooling at the factory? Why buy an antique that was hardly two weeks old?

The chaotic layout of the warehouse led many customers to believe they might, in some obscure corner, find a rare treasure, overlooked by others. But all this old stuff was absolutely brand-new; we carried special crayons in our pockets to keep it that way, coloring in the scratches before we showed people their purchases. These people wanted old furniture but perfect, they wanted antiques without time. Still, the animating urge, the desire for the real wasn't dead; the day I started the job I noticed nobody bought from the top, no one purchased the front item. Looking behind, for these people, equaled searching for the past, the authentic. Picky, savvy shoppers always made their selections by searching deep into the stacks and piles, mistrusting the surface, the present appearance of things.

Maybe nostalgia is a species of the ideal, a dream of a last interior, where all the commotion of a life is finally rewarded with rest, drained of history. We were selling the memory of something, of hard work and industry, of necessity, of craft and artisanship—the mendacious idea that life was gathered with greater force and organized in superior ways in the past. People were hungry for the attributes of hardship, and our faux antiques replaced the real past with an emblematic one. Or something. I could never quite untwist the riddle completely. When you stood in the warehouse the eye was pleasantly bombarded by a vastness filled. But the inspiration for most of the furniture we sold came originally from hardscrabble times, times of scarcity and unrest and an economy based on need, not surplus, and certainly not this absurd superfluity, this crazy proliferation, where two hundred oak iceboxes, stacked to the ceiling on layers of cardboard, would easily sell out on a Saturday afternoon.

After closing I'd slip a padlock in the loading-dock door, then stay inside: the furniture warehouse was also my home. I lived in there, vaguely employed as a night watchman. Every night I slept on one of, I'm guessing, two hundred sofas. I ate take-out dinners on tables that would be sold the next day. I read books by the greenish light of an ugly banker's lamp, set on a fake oak icebox. My boss was a man of great good fortune who liked to squire his mistress around town in a restored Model T Ford. He hired me to deter theft, set out glue traps, and hose down the Dumpsters so bums wouldn't light the cardboard on fire, trying to keep warm. I simplified my job by rigging a cheap alarm system out of magnetic triggers and a hundred yards of lamp wire and a couple of Radio Shack sirens perched on the windowsills. In the evenings I'd arm the thing by twisting together the exposed copper strands and head next door to my uncle's bar.

You entered the bar through a black door with a diamond peephole. There were nine stools covered in red leatherette. My uncle did book and collected numbers. Among the patrons you found a deep well of faith, a certain gut feel for what Catholic theologians would call "analogical thinking," whereby you come to know the reality of God through signs. Gambling was how you negotiated the tricky path between situation and symbol. Winning was always an answer to a question. Most of the men were spooky about the stool they sat on and would rather stand all night than take a seat that had somehow been hoodooed by past bad luck. Many of these gamblers were afraid of the past, haunted by it, and this tilted their faith in the direction of fate, a less ample, less accommodating idea. On any given night thousands of bloated dollars would sit on the bar in wet, frowning stacks. I'd never seen such sums. I drank Old Style and peppermint schnapps and lived off pork rinds and pickled eggs. The eggs floated in a gallon jar of green amniotic pond water like specimens of some kind of nascent life form.

Gambling and dim light and slow-rising smoke and the forgottenness of the place made it seem like everybody in the bar had strange and compelling mysteries behind them. They were dense with background, or so you inferred, or romanticized, because the present, the very surface of life, was so meager, so without evidence or account. The bar was the kind of place where people were "characters" and were known, to the extent that they were known at all, by some fragment of personality, a piece of self broken off and magnified until it was more recognizable than the original man behind it, overshadowing him. Character, in the bar, really was fate.

And so a character named Red Devil seemed a proxy voice, speaking for everybody, when he would cackle hysterically and yell out, "Manteno, 1963. I'm history!" Manteno was the state mental hospital but nothing beyond that was elaborated. To be history in America doesn't mean to be recorded, noted, added to the narrative, but precisely the opposite, to be gone, banished, left behind. To be history is to be cut from the story.

Other characters? Here are two. They even have character names, names I'd avoid if I were writing fiction: Al and George.

Al tended the bar at night. He'd been in the merchant marine and ate with a fat clunky thumb holding down his plate, as if he were afraid the whole place might pitch and yaw and send his dinner flying. He was dwarfish and looked like an abandoned sculpture, a forgotten intention. His upper body was a slablike mass, a plinth upon which his head rested; he had a chiseled nose and jaw, a hack-job scar of a mouth; his hands were thick and stubby, more like paws than anything prehensile. Sitting back behind the bar, smoking Pall Malls, he seemed petrified, the current shape of his body achieved by erosion, his face cut by clumsy strokes and blows. His eyes, though, were soft and blue, always wet and weepy with rheum, and when you looked at Al, you had the disorienting sense of something trapped, something fluid and human caught inside the gray stone vessel of his gargoyle body, gazing out through those eyes. He was my only real neighbor. At closing he'd collect the glasses, wipe down the bottles, shut the blinds, and go to sleep on the bar. In the morning he'd fold his blankets and stow them away in a cardboard box.

George was another fixture in the bar, a salesman working, like me, in the furniture warehouse. He drank beer all day, chased with shots of peppermint schnapps so that his breath would smell fresh, as though he'd just brushed his teeth. Like most drunks he had the baffling notion he was getting away with it, fooling everybody. I felt sorry for George because he wasn't fooling anybody and couldn't see the truth, that he was being tolerated and temporarily ignored. With his insulin shots, instant coffee, his shabby dress, his elaborate comb-over, he led an obscure life, irregular and unobserved, except at the bar. There he gambled with a nervousness torqued up tight by a belief in the quick tidy fate of accidents, of moments that decide everything. Sometime in the past, he believed, things had gone wrong, gone fatally so. The present was his evidence. Divorce. Bankruptcy. Alcoholism. He had a gimpy leg, he was diabetic. He gambled the games, the horses, the numbers, the state lottery, everything. Sometime in the future there was a wager that would be won, a score that would redress everything, and perhaps this injection of faith, more than, say, a visit to the doctor, eased the pain for him.

"When I have money," he told me, "I can't sleep, I can't hardly eat. I don't feel good until it's gone."

In the bar a small bet was called "an interest bet," a wager that attached you fiercely, with greater vividness, to the flow of an otherwise monotonous day. It offered you a way into time, via the wide and democratic avenue of chance; even the smallest gamble instantly gave you a stake in the outcome of time itself. With a bet on, time had something to show you, held the promise of a revelation. When George was betting he had the sensibility of a psychotic, or a poet. There were nuances to assay, meanings to consider. Accidents became auguries. The odds on unrelated matters changed. Emotions rose to the surface, the buried inner life became relevant, and he grew sensitive, tender, his instinctual self, now resuscitated, engaged in the world's new density. Nothing out in the actual world demanded quite the same concentration of being, the same focused energy. With money on the line, he became aware of time, of his place in it, and planned ahead. On payday he broke half his check into quarters, dimes, and nickels, storing the coins in a coffee can at home; it was the only way he could keep himself from gambling all his money and make sure he'd have enough saved aside for food at the end of the month.

Most people in the area around the bar were passing through, transient. They were commuters who caught the trains and left behind an acute emptiness, a hollow around seven o'clock every night. Of course some people came in search of precisely this lacuna, this moment when the day lapsed into nothingness. Richard Speck sought it, holing up at the Starr Hotel a few blocks away, paying ninety cents a night for his furnished room, in the weeks after he'd murdered eight student nurses. This was 1966 and Speck planned to hop a freight train west but never managed to leave the Loop until he was sentenced to death. The single nurse who survived that attack, hidden flat beneath a bed, figured in my dreams for years. She squeezed herself beneath that bed and for hours listened to the sounds of sex followed by the sounds of death. I was a very young boy when this proto-horrific crime happened but for some reason I know Speck tenderly asked the last woman he was raping if she'd wrap her legs around him. That winter they tore down the Starr Hotel and I watched from a distance, watched the swing of a wrecking ball as it arced through the air, collided soundlessly, then came through, a couple of seconds later, with a laggard explosion of crumbling brick.

At night, black men in jalopy flatbeds scavenged through mounds of debris to save the bricks. In a book about brick, D. Knickerbacker Boyd writes: "When two bricks are struck together, they should emit a metallic ring." That's true. Bricks clink together with a satisfying ring akin to fine crystal. The sound has a clarity, a rightness. Bricks also improve with age, and highly valued skids of cured Chicago brick were sold to people as far away as Phoenix and San Francisco, people who made walkways, garden walls, and barbecues from remnants of old factories. At night the air cleared of dust. To the west was Greektown, across the freeway, with a row of restaurants concentrated enough so that some nights I'd pick up the arid scent of oregano; north was the Haymarket with its rotting fruit; and from somewhere, on certain nights, in a building I searched for but could never locate, a candymaker spread the smell of chocolate and cinnamon in the air. From my window in the warehouse I'd hear the black men knocking away like moonlighting archaeologists, knocking until the old soft mortar was chipped loose and the clean red brick rang out as resonantly as a bell.

In the bar people kept drinking and betting right up to the very end. One night a stranger appeared and took George by the arm and led him gently, like a church usher, out to the sidewalk. Words were exchanged in pantomime. After a minute the stranger crushed George in the head with a length of pipe. George had raised his arms in supplication, beseeching, and when the pipe crashed down his head bowed penitentially before he slumped to his knees, then fell forward on his face. You hardly ever see adults on the ground, they don't spin or twirl, they don't flop over and fall for the fun of it, not like kids. In my experience adults went to the ground only in death. George owed the man money. It was a confusing sight, seeing him like that, a grown man sprawled out on the sidewalk, small and broken, with no more control over himself than a child.

Now when I think of it, I understand it was never so much the potential for gain that animated gamblers like George, these men who had nothing, but being reawakened to a world where loss was once again possible. That's really what gave them life and drove them again and again to the game. Loss was their métier and to have that taken away, to be, finally, lost, was the worst thing imaginable. As long as you could fall farther you distinguished yourself from the fallen. Loss reinstated possibility, but possibility without hope. And perhaps this explains how all of us blithely imagined that the general wreckage would pass over the bar, that it was somehow exempt. Gambling offered a refuge from the outside world, its advances, its mysterious evolution. No one believed the bar would end, not because we didn't believe in progress, but instead, more precisely, because our kind of gambling, the wish of it, was an attempt to salvage the past. We weren't so much hoping to change the future as we were trying to amend history. We wanted the past completely restored and made livable. We believed that was the only kind of winning that counted. ❖

Hell House

Hell House is a ramshackle arrangement of buildings meant to depict in a literal and somewhat medieval way the vast potential for ending up eternally damned. It's a haunted house in a haunted world, and through it you wind, down corridors of billowing black Visqueen, through rooms luridly lit by strobes and TV screens, past stage sets peopled with rapists and murderers and terrorists until, briefly interred in a black coffin whose convenient and clever back door opens onto the afterlife, some souls ascend into heaven while most are dragged down to hell. It's an eschatological vision made up of a by-now-familiar triad of fundamentalism, outsized Texas bullshit, and some of the lowest conservative clichés about life in the big bad world—basically an undiluted version of our president[1], and as such, I guess, the potshots have already been taken. One hates to go to hell only to come back scoffing, but I took the tour three or four times, on two different nights, and the miscellanea of horror that made up this particular rendition lacked anguish and torment, not to mention the visceral, abreacted thrills you expect a good haunted house to have. There was a sort of moral hauteur that irritated me, but I was really hoping for spooky lowbrow sleights along the lines of peeled grapes for eyeballs and clumps of cold spaghetti for brains and whatnot. A major failing of Hell House was simply that it wasn't scary.

Physical fear is more immediately threatening than the far-off rumored torments of damnation, and Hell House might have found a more effective model had it based itself on the annual hazing of pledges and cadets or the ordeal of grunts at a Marine Corps boot camp. I went to an all-boys school and for Frosh Week was made to sit in a tub of shit and lettuce, filled to the brim with fetid water and stirred with an oar, surrounded by crazed, shouting, doped-up seniors, and that was more unbearably nightmarish than any of the cornball lessons about moral hygiene I got from Hell House. Bodily fear just isn't rejectable, whereas moral

---

1 W. Bush at the time of writing.

and religious ideas, Pentecostal or Catholic, right or left, are better handled by hermeneutics than horror, and anyway should operate under different rules of suasion. That conversion is sometimes accomplished brutally and by subjection ought to be seen as aberrant and a sad lapse, a drop in the level of discourse. But hazing, with its disorientation, its deprivations, is fairly nondenominational. You don't need to evangelize in order to persuade. You confuse the senses, you tilt a floor, you dead-end a few of the dark corridors, you create prolonged silences, you flash white lights bright enough to blind, you blast noise so loudly stout men faint, you suffuse a room with the sulfurous reek of rotten eggs, you set up a gallery of yucky tactile experiences, you tease out a taste of eternity in a coffin with a claustrophobic stay in a closet, you do that and I really doubt the morality of abortion or homosexuality, for instance, would be half as worrisome, at least not for the immediate duration.

In other words, the argument of a haunted house ought to be aimed at the human body. In that sense, it should be morally neutral, or neutralizing. A good haunted house is about the utter collapse of our accidental differences, the uselessness of class, of gender, of education, of personal history, of all the distinctions we cobble together and call the self. Late enough at night none of this stuff protects you, not from the boogey-man. What's haunted or, more accurately, what's uncovered by terror, is the poor forked thing, and the agon of a haunted house isn't between God and Satan, or the righteous and the sinners, but rather between the self and annihilation. Horror resembles humor in its leveling capacity, although the anesthetic quality of comedy, its coldness toward bodily pain, is replaced in a moment of fear by a more complete and nearby peril. If comedy is somehow about the body as an unfeeling object, then fear is the surge of feeling into a body threatened with nonbeing. A haunted house poses ontological problems, and thus ought to place courage in jeopardy—it ought to reach down deep into the Platonic dualism between physical and spiritual courage and blast it apart. A good haunting gives us a workable vision of equality, a denominator similar to the *danse macabre*. It's probably fair to speculate that medieval depictions of putrefaction, particularly of worms crawling out of the bowels, drew inspiration from the visceral experience of fear, its locus in the upset stomach, which feels wormy when one is frightened, and to the extent that Hell House retained its folkloric roots it might have tapped that primitive seat of horror. A haunted house makes the experience of horror real, a thing inescapably participated in, with everybody hell-bound. But too often Hell House made the mistake of locating fear elsewhere, referring to moral arguments and social issues outside its walls and, in doing so, letting the drama of the endangered body drain away. Like it or not, a haunted house is a sensual affair, more like sex than theology, and won't survive too much abstract organization or the damping down of strangeness and intuition, of otherness or the mystery of skin or whatever. Hell House didn't obliterate distinctions and categories but erected them, the better to separate the saints from the sinners, at the expense of good fun. That a tour of hell would end in a call to prayer indicates the problem—if it had been more elemental and troubling, I would have come out the other end in need of water or air or sedatives.

Each room in Hell House could be considered a canto in the *Commedia*, particularly the *Inferno*, except that the idea of descent in Dante, the funneled shape of hell as you circle down into worse and worse sins, was ditched by Hell House in favor of a cosmologically flat canvas in which all sins were equally bad, and the entire trip instead resembled the morality plays and pageants put on for the feast of Corpus Christi in the fourteenth century. I'm not so much talking about design or construction here as the religious arrangement of sins. In that sense it stepped back from the Renaissance and the availability of perspective into the depthless stage of Everyman in the late Middle Ages. As a moral program, the schema for Hell House was linear, but as a physical structure, as architecture, it was anfractuous, like an intestine, twisting and turning, kinked here and there with knots, and the tour took you not so much down, as toward, an interior. It wasn't actually a house; it was more like visiting a sin zoo, strolling from room to room, watching the curious habits of fucked-up people. In each of the seven or so rooms you saw a playlet but there was no overall narrative. The entire visit lasted about an hour, but with no plot, no torquing up of the drama, I arrived at the Day of Judgment bored to death.

You were ushered through Hell House by ghouls in skull masks and black capes. Some of the ghouls wore tennis shoes and were obviously adolescent, and their taunting had a certain playground aspect that was really annoying and bratty. There were even some especially short skinny ghouls no older than nine or ten or eleven who, relaxing between acts with their hoods off, came at me and the photographer, as we dawdled behind our group, and told us to go to hell, pointing the way. "Go to hell!" they kept saying, over and over, obviously enjoying a curse that, for the two-week run of Hell House, was officially sanctioned. As the tour went on it became clear to me that these ghouls were quite specifically the voice of conservative values, although at first it had seemed as if they were supposed to incarnate the devil himself. Either way, these kids qua ghouls weren't giving off a full human vibration.

The tour took you through a variety of rooms, all staged like a theatrical set: the cabin of a jetliner, a rave, a hospital, a garage, a family room, a burial site, a cult sacrifice, a living room, a coffin, heaven, hell, and, before finally releasing you to the cold Dallas night and a cup of hot chocolate at the concession stand, a place to pray and perhaps even convert. Each room held its corresponding sin, the exact nature of which was often elusive. Loosely, you saw drugs plus sex, abortion plus sex, a slumber party plus sex plus murder, a cult sacrifice plus drugs plus murder, porno plus promiscuity plus bastardy plus sodomy plus suicide, and so on—there was a tendency to pile on and the impression was that you couldn't sin casually or recreationally but had to be hardcore and committed.

The audience watched as a group, from behind a cordon. A few examples should suffice to give a flavor of the whole. The set for the Abortion Scene was a hospital room. A girl in blue scrubs was wheeled in on a gurney, her crotch and thighs garishly soaked in blood. She screamed her head off while a doctor and nurse talked across the gurney, consulting so calmly and in such quiet voices they seemed to belong to another story entirely. Whoever wrote the script hadn't labored much over their dialogue—they showed no concern. You stared right at the girl's spread legs—I did, anyway—and that was weird. Her positioning sexualized the moment grotesquely—the bath of blood and the girl's agonal cries and even her death were an obvious but sick and grossly caricatured loss of virginity. More important, though, the girl's death was an act of revenge, it was retribution for killing an unborn child. It proved a conservative moral point—all the while she was dying the ghouls leaned over the gurney and ridiculed her.

The Slumber Party Scene involved two girls having a sleepover, listening to Mariah Carey, watching television and talking about what they'd like to be when they grow up. Then a man breaks into the house and abducts one of the girls, taking her to his car for what he calls "fun." You hear one of the ghouls say: "Don't you just love the smell of fresh meat?"—which totally threw off the point of view for me. Up to that moment my sympathy had been entirely with the girls, but now the ghoul seemed to be saying that this young woman, hauled off to be raped, had somehow invited the moment, had transgressed, was blameworthy. Suddenly the ghoul was an agent of justice. Why else make this observation about fresh meat? It was creepy. Throughout Hell House it was mostly (sexual) girls who were in jeopardy, owing in part, I suppose, to the stock conventions of horror flicks; the girls' bodies acted as territory in a disputed moral landscape. In the very next scene, which took place in a roofless structure, semi-outdoors, you see the same girl roped to a joist, her hands tied above her head, while her abductor digs the hole he plans to dump her body in.

In the Porno Scene, we see this slumpy guy on a couch, watching dirty movies. His girlfriend comes home. She tells him she's pregnant. Then she tells him the child she's carrying isn't his; it's his best friend's. Then he violently forces some kind of humiliating sex on her. (We segue from the living room to the bedroom by watching a black-and-white video, quite blurry, that suggests rough stuff.) The acting in these skits, by the way, was a mixed bag, ranging from OK to horrible, but many of the girls, when they had to scream, could really belt it out. It was never the scream of a real person in real pain but rather a homage to horror movies. When the boyfriend leaves, the girl curses, giving the very best, full-out scream of the whole tour, rolls on the floor, blasphemously accusing her Bible and God of abandonment, and eventually kills herself, simulating slashed wrists by popping a plastic ampoule of stage blood, quite convincingly, on her arm.

All of this was meant to be hideous and repellent, yet each room offered such a long, prurient, gazing look into the life of degradation that the scenarios often seemed like a spastic reaction against a real desire, a fascination. I see two ways to take this observation. One is: somewhere along the line somebody had to imagine the act of sex, and that's one of the reasons, I think, that so many of the stories ended in murder—it was a way of punishing the imagination and paying for the fundamentalist sin of passing sympathy. The economy of it was creepy in its efficiency, with the condemnation and dispatch following so swiftly on the lapse or frailty or doubt, never considering, for instance, that promiscuity might be about an ambivalent need for love, or the desire, the stray hope, for something other than nothing—possibilities that would engage the imagination, tempting it. And the other is: no one ever actually imagined any of this and Hell House was, instead, a gathering of clichés whose entelechy was fear and this house, far from being haunted, was in fact a safe refuge from the morally confusing universe out beyond the walls of black plastic. The sins were all childishly obvious, and I was aware, just vaguely, of being catechized. Very often I felt the tour wasn't about conversion but enlistment, and as such, it was a test of loyalty, with anyone who was the slightest bit recreant banished. Loyalty—in its darkest form, which left so much death as its legacy to the twentieth century—rids the divided self of anxiety and guilt, so that murder smiles. The ghouls in Hell House did a lot of gloating as others suffered.

There was a dispirited familiarity to the rooms, a lack of care about the shabby way things looked. Most of the furniture, I imagine, came from thrift stores, arriving at Hell House pre-saddened by other lives, other misfortunes. Everything lacked an element of choice, the memory of an original moment of hope about how things would be. The interiors were decidedly lower middle-class. The headboard in the porn scene was flimsy, not up to the rigors of a good sodomizing, and the vanity was one of those things that put you in mind of a wedding cake, white and elaborate and frilly, so vestal and princessy you just know heartbreak is in store for any girl still holding on to those misplaced hopes past the age of twelve. Things were sad as gesture, sad as furniture, in a world premised on the idea that appearance is a lie. The percale sheets, the sagging mattress, the framed art on the walls (because *art* is what a blank wall wants), all of it lacked vitality. The sofa was slouchy and vague as to color and the various easy chairs were worn and soiled and the carpet was the kind that's already there when you move in, with faint paths turned pale where other people have walked. It was a décor that suggested hope was elsewhere, in another life, and a décor that suggested unseen enemies, the sort of place that feels shameful and mean in a world where the failure to prosper is a sin. Of course, the sets were meant to exist only gesturally, as props, but there was something in the hard literal fact, in their mere presence, that encouraged you to see them in a realistic mode. The dingy and dim rooms made for an atmosphere of sordid involvement—they were meant to indicate a shabby moral state, a despondency—but to me the "sins" did not seem moral so much as economic and aesthetic—a matter of both failed consumption and poor taste. Hopelessness had come to reside in the sofa on the porn set because it would never move again, because time had come for it and stayed, like an intimation of death. You felt nothing would change, that progress was gone and destiny mislaid; what the future held was repetition and sameness. There was a malignancy in this world, but it wasn't a problem you could blame on the devil. In Hell House it wasn't sin so much as sadness and despair and heartbreak and misfortune and cluelessness and just every stupid human possibility that was answered with damnation. People pathetically in need of help were shot.

And so as we wandered from room to room, every narrative ended in death, every story came to the same conclusion, until it felt as if a flawed and fallen world were finally being cleaned up and organized and made perfect. Mistakes were made, and the mistaken were efficiently condemned, leaving behind empty squalid rooms in which it was impossible to imagine a tender unseen moment or a kind word or a shared silence that wasn't murderous. It's perhaps needless to say, but the people in these skits lacked a living texture, were crude-minded and ugly in spirit and, in general, dismissively drawn. Hell House resembled the smutty mood of a sixties exploitation film more than religion, a spectacle of types, lewd and overblown, exaggerated to the point of pornography with its parade of stock characters. But Hell House was quite specifically somebody's vision of others. Whoever created Hell House seemed to despise people, their freedom, the varied possibility of them. Whoever it was could imagine only concluded lives, lives summed up by a single act, in a world where most of us have agreed, not always happily, to live with ambiguity. Every fundamentalism focuses on end times, and Armageddon is, in a sense, a rhetorical trope, an emphatic and overwhelming conclusion, meant to wrap up and make tidy the mistaken wanderings of history. For a fundamentalist the end is one of the forms desire takes, a passion no different from lust or avarice, intense with longing and the need for fulfillment and relief. It's like they're horny for apocalypse. They get off on denouements, which partly explains why Hell House never amounted to much more than a series of murderous conclusions. It focused only on that part of a story where life finds itself fated. Inside every act a judgment was coiled. Real people, with their ragged and uncertain lives, their stumbling desires, their bleak or blessed futures, would only break into the narrative, complicating the story, dragging it on endlessly.

You would think there'd be enormous anxiety involved in desiring the end since the end doesn't seem to actually be anything. And perhaps it's the messed-up management of this anxiety that accounts for Hell House's failure. Kierkegaard says anxiety "is altogether different from fear and similar concepts that refer to something definite." He says, "anxiety is freedom's actuality as the possibility of possibility." In other words, anxiety has no object; in fact, it tries to become fear because fear has a definite object that can be faced with courage. I think it's fair to say horror bridges some kind of gap between fear and anxiety, using objects that are present yet unreal, objects that retain a somewhat objectless character. Horror makes visible the source of our anxiety, typically arriving dressed as death. It's nothingness in a black cloak, coming for all of us, a bequest of our bodies. But Hell House was premised on an antipathy to the suddenly helpless body, a hatred. It gutted the very thing that would make it compelling. Instead of indulging the thrills inherent to horror, it swapped out anxiety for fear and came up with morality as an answer to annihilation. The hated content of Hell House was arrived at via a bunch of rejections, a denial, a suppression of the self, which helped the creator form a superiority over the rest of us who are slogging our way—living and loving, doubting and sorrowing—toward a hole in the dirt. The Pentecostals who created Hell House converted their anxiety over the human body into persecution, and their horror set them dreaming of death.

Added up, room plus room plus room, Hell House was a holocaust. Everybody died. They died—they were killed off—because they lived the wrong way, made the wrong choices, believed and thought or felt the wrong things. The whole thing kind of sickened me. The last night I stood outside, absurdly thinking of Dante and his imagery, as the kids rehearsed their lines in the early dark before Hell House officially opened. Out on the lawn you heard a disembodied anguished call in the cold: "Where am I? What's going on?" And the strange music of a young girl warming her voice with: "God hates you. You killed your baby. I hear babies crying." I stood for a while in a field, listening, then went inside to inspect

the Rosco fog machine that would make Heaven the
ethereal stuff of visions and the Styrofoam rock where,
in half an hour, a sinner would be chained for eternity.
The rooms lost nothing for being empty. In the hospital
the bloodstained gurney waited for what the script called
"The Abortion Girl," a name as allegorical as Bunyan's
Giant Despair. The sacks of plasma hung from their IV
poles, the false charts were clamped into their clipboards,
the stethoscope waited for its heart. The Abortion Girl
would again scream and hemorrhage and die hideously
a dozen or more times later that night, and again her
nightmarish pain would be mocked, but for now an accepting silence held the room. In the Garage Scene, the
paint cans, the Hefty sacks twisted at the neck, the red
car, all of it was stubbornly real in a way the stilted dialogue would not be. In the Slumber Party Scene, soon
enough, the raped girl would hang from her rope, the
abductor would dig his hole. But the show hadn't begun yet and there was no morality or condemnation just
now. The shovel was there and so was the partially dug
grave and the heap of overturned dirt smelled wet and
loamy and the rope dangled, empty and waiting, as a
light rain fell through the roof. It was beautiful, and a
relief, mostly a relief, to feel the rain coming down and
know how resistant reality was, how durable, even in a
world drained of love. ❖

One More Paradise

In a story about paradise, the complications inevitably follow, so perhaps a simple description first—Biosquat is three or four acres of scrub, a derelict tract of land in East Austin (itself a somewhat neglected section of the city) on which Dave Santos has established at least the rudiments of an eco-village. There's a cattle gate and a mailbox out front, and a forked tote road leads partway into the property; from there footpaths wind through stands of juniper and oak and mesquite. Plants in this part of the country, baffled by the sun, seek and hide from it all at once, suffering a kind of conflicted heliotropism in which the branches of a dry fissured oak, for instance, grow up and out, turn back, go down, curl and twist, writhing so much that, even still, they seem in motion, snaking like the hair of a Gorgon. The heat in August is oppressive, and the umbrage these stunted trees provide is spotty, more shadow than shade, offering little relief. Underfoot, the blanched soil at Biosquat feels like crushed brick and hardly seems arable. I saw no wildlife other than a few lizards, although I was told rats and raccoons, as well as coral snakes, live in the area. Mosquitoes were plague-plentiful, and Dave Santos suggested, rather alarmingly, that the once-numerous crows were decimated by West Nile virus. In the distance you could hear the constant hum of cars, and while Biosquat's ambitions are somewhat Edenic, at present it still retains the mood and look of a vacant lot; it has a spurned and forgotten quality, as if the world had, without warning or explanation, fallen in love with someone else.

Once inside the gate, along the paths, you find the first improvements, the nets and tents and bamboo beds, the solar panels and the cistern and the terraced gardens, a limestone megalith surrounded by rickety scaffolds and a series of unfinished structures, the ceilings of which are fabricated from bike rims and a cladding of placards and signs left behind by old political campaigns. There's a pale green trailer and a toilet mounted on a tricycle and a trellis of unripe tomatoes hanging, again, from bike rims. There's welding equipment, there's rebar and conduit, there's an anvil on a stump and a primitive garden hoe cleverly forged from a piece of pipe and a chain ring. The visual impact of the place is surreal and collagist, although, sprawling with junk, it also comes quite close in character to the sort of illegal dump site every city has, those wooded hillsides that mysteriously fill with unwanted mattresses and shopping carts and washing machines. Over the couple of hot August days I spent at Biosquat, Santos often spoke of "trash worship," an idea meant to elevate debris into an aesthetic and invigorate refuse with a rarefied sense of social mission—something more high-minded and messianic than recycling, at any rate—and perhaps that's what he's up to, perhaps the bikes and the rebar and the bamboo aren't haphazard, aren't just old crap nobody else wants, but are instead the base materials for building the small, resonant civilization he imagines.

I, for one, was willing to believe. I was willing to believe that, on a warm fall night in the future, estivating frogs would bellow to life in ponds that, as of now, don't exist. I was willing to believe that human shit is second only to bat guano as a nutrient and fertilizer, and that it's entirely odorless when mixed with mulch. I was willing to believe that a recipe of soybean oil and chili peppers would eradicate the mosquitoes and make for an edible pesticide. I was willing to believe in things I did not understand, in Hilbert space and eigenforms and combinatorics, and I was willing to believe in houses that would someday look, fantastically, like big puppets. I was more than willing to believe in a world in which, quite beautifully, nothing was outcast or lost or abandoned, not people or things or ideals. I was willing to believe in all the enthusiasms Dave Santos believes in—the radical circus and the mutant bikes and the chicken tractor and the gnat goggles and the flying robots and the car that runs on rain. I was even willing to believe, in principle, that an earthly paradise, lush and complete, could be improvised and sustained with rainwater, PVC pipe, a homemade cistern, and a solar-powered bilge pump. I was willing to believe all of this and more—that human migration and nomadism make sense, that pedaling a bike a mere six weeks a year will keep you in an eternal spring, that Bucky Fuller once bathed a family of four with a single cup of water—but I was not willing to believe this:

"Ultimately, I think colonizing the atmosphere is the solution to a lot of ecological problems . . . [*Uh-huh.*][1] And it's also more sensible than the space fantasies— the idea that we're ready to build a bunch of rockets and blast off and live in orbit. [*Right.*] Engineering-wise,

---

1 My questions and exclamations—every noise I made—appear here within brackets.

it's much simpler to colonize the lower atmosphere. [*Uh-huh.*] And so we have the stratosphere, is where I started theorizing. I lectured at UT Aerospace on the subject . . . We could take carbon out of the atmosphere. We have excess carbon dioxide, we'd liberate oxygen to help us breathe up in the stratosphere, we could mix that oxygen in with our helium and live inside these huge cathedral spaces—we'd be talking a little like Donald Duck—but because of the solar energy coming in we'd have a shirtsleeve, close-to-sea-level-pressure environment, up above the weather [*Uh-huh.*], and totally reliable electric solar power. [*Yeah.*] And we could use that electricity for ion propulsion to crack the carbon dioxide, to regenerate the ozone, using the catalytic reactors of these ion propulsion engines, and get carbon credits, from, like, the nations that want to do something good for the environment. We could build this aerial civilization from the carbon we've dumped in the atmosphere. [*Yeah, yeah.*]

"And then go anywhere we want, like the round-the-world ballooners. By knowing, by being able to visualize the atmosphere, they can steer . . . [*Uh-huh.*] And they didn't even have any propulsion except the ability to go up and down. [*Right. Right. Right, right.*] So we have these sites around the world that are like stratospheric elevators where prevailing winds hit a mountain and create a stratospheric mountain wave, and so those are places you could have gliders that soar up to your stratospheric cities. [*Yeah.*] Getting down's easy. [*Right.*] You could just skydive. [*Uh-huh.*] Out of the stratosphere. [*Yeah, yeah.*] It would be the basis of an Olympian civilization, living up in the clouds. I'd like to see socially conscious hippies get there as opposed to some death star. [*Yeah, yeah, yeah—so you see Biosquat in relation to everything you're saying as . . .*] As a stepping-stone. [*Yeah—it also seems somehow, uh, it seems very fluid.*]"

Dave Santos has some higher education, but essentially he's a kind of autodidact. He went to Washington College ("a party school on the great waterbird migratory flyway of the Chesapeake"), dropped out, enrolled at the University of Texas, dropped out, matriculated, dropped out, whereafter he cut tuition costs by auditing classes or simply sitting in on lectures that interested him. ("I was able to lap up aura and knowledge from Nobel laureates and other legends in this way.") In conversation he has that ravenous fierce range of the self-taught: Hilbert space, Foucault, ion propulsion, Hazlitt's translation of Montaigne, heuristic programming, Rousseau in the original French ("It wore me out."), matrix algebra, zines, Mircea Eliade, Radio Shack manuals, predicate calculus, pamphlets on composting. Without much lingering or elaboration the learned references pile up—some Foucault here, a little Rousseau over there—in an allusive, jumbled analogue to the vacant lot Biosquat is built on. For Santos—fringy, wandering outside the codes and canons of academe—every book he's read is a perfect, remarkable *objet trouvé*, to which he brings tremendous zeal.

Like a lot of autodidacts, Dave Santos wants to outsmart you. His language sounds impressively academic but slightly forged. He favors, for instance, coinages ("biobikes," "edjidotopia"), as if he were exploring the frontiers of a discipline, working a lonely terrain and discovering things for which, as yet, there are no names; or he dresses up a phrase for the scientifically credible sound it will make ("Arrest Proofing Protocols," "Bivy Head Observatory"); and whenever there is an opportunity to swap in a complex word for a simple one, an elaborate construction for a clear explanation, Santos is there, substituting "rear-optics" for mirror, "micro-hedonics" for good fun, and "dive reflex" for hitting the ditch, creating his own taxonomy, a systematics behind which, I suspect, there is no system.

This makes him powerful and persuasive to a point, and never less than entertaining, but I think too that his showy, protesting intelligence masks an insecurity, a feeling, never entirely put to rest, that he doesn't belong in the room. He talked about attending AI conferences with his home-built robots and being "respected by these people who, normally, without a PhD, you shouldn't even be in the same room [with]." "Shouldn't" is a curious choice—why not the more neutral "couldn't" or "wouldn't"?—in that the word subtly switches the speaker: it doesn't actually belong to Santos but to the voice of an absent, unnamed, scolding authority. Here, then, is the central theme of paradise—banishment and exile.

And so in exile—let's say—he elaborates his own thing. The various structures on Biosquat proper include the sleeping quarters, mostly tents and mosquito netting, and "the mother ship," as Santos calls it, a travel trailer the color of canned peas that sits under a carport. The trailer is rough and shabby, the kitchen kind of a sty, ruling out any chance that Biosquat has a hidden desire for conventional uptight domestic order. All of this is fairly standard, and the cheap, sagging tents in particular give the place the familiar look and feel of a homeless camp. The chicken tractor is interesting—a low cage laid out along a footpath, with a plywood coop at one end. The idea is that the chickens, confined to a run, will peck and till the earth, kill the weeds, eat the insects, shit and thereby fertilize the soil, but just before I arrived they

were depredated by raccoons (dramatizing a flaw in the
curious harmonic stasis of Eden that I could never resolve in childhood: What would everybody eat, I'd wonder, if they couldn't eat each other?) A homemade cistern
collects water from the roof of the carport; the water is
then pumped to the terraced gardens, and a solar oven,
sitting on a shopping cart—a corolla of petal-shaped
panels open to the sun—generates just enough heat to
cook a pot of beans.

The most interesting structures at Biosquat are built
with an armature of bike rims sheathed with corrugated
plastic. The rims are fastened together with tie wire and
arch nicely toward the sky, propped up from below by
lengths of bent rebar or the trunks of scavenged trees.
The chrome spokes make for exactly the kind of airi-
ness Santos seeks elsewhere through elevated language;
their thinness gives an otherwise stout ceiling a delicate appearance and, clad with the corrugated plastic,
which is predominantly white, the rims and spokes together look, overhead, like a drove of gauzy parasols.
The curving shape and the texture of the skin remind
you of Gehry, as does the collagist sensibility and the
use Santos makes of cheap-tech materials. At this point
in their construction, somewhat unfinished, you feel
like calling these ingenious, junky, Quonset-like things
"pieces"—as you would a piece of sculpture. It's one of

the paradoxes I found most intriguing about Santos: that he's a commissioned sculptor, working in an art form bound to materials and materiality while putting such a heavy, personal accent on ideas of ascent and the ethereal. This isn't an ambition foreign to sculpture, for sure, and even straight verisimilitude is an attempt to lift life out of stone, transcending a basic, obdurate fact about the physical stuff. So the pieces are unfinished—although given their resemblance to collage and their use of trash they may always resist looking finished—and in their present condition they encapsulate the cosmology of Santos's project as a whole. There's the empyreal ceiling above, shaped like a parachute, and then, below, Santos is building rude walls from red clay that he digs out of the ground; in between, the walls will be reinforced using, of course, bike frames—a sort of colorful bike rebar that, at this point, remains exposed, so that the bikes emerge from the clay and sit at a sort of midpoint between earth and sky.

Flight is a leitmotif for Santos, and the theme reaches richly into all the word's meanings, from flying to fleeing to the exuberances of fancy and transcendence to joyrides and quests. "You need that metaphoric inspiration to get a focus," he says. And so when he talks of nomadism the idea veers from roving bikes to migratory birds and eventually melds into "a dream of autonomous migration in self-sufficient skybikes with ultralight amenities. It is a soaring of light spirits—dematerialized, floating, ethereal, intense." A skybike probably should not "dematerialize," not in flight, anyway, but it's the turning of this kind of trope that marks for me the line between belief and disbelief, between accepting the visionary and balking at the vision. The movement from skybikes as an engineering feat to light spirits as a condition of the soul is purely metaphoric. It owes more to the Book of Revelation than it does to physics, more to the ecstatic tradition in poetry than it does to aeronautics. Looking around Biosquat, at the tangle of bikes or the hardscrabble soil, the effort of translating stubborn matter into an immaterial vision is evident. It's slow going. And while the freedom described here is a spiritual event—an apotheosis—it's also an escape from the poverty of the corporeal world, a gripe you always hear from lyric poets, saints, and visionaries.

This is tricky terrain, the transition from the airy intensity of the imagination to the denser inspissations of reality. In his writings on the web Santos so often leaves sense for sound, so often eases away from the meaning of a word for the music it will make and abandons practicality for the pleasing image, that his real project seems to be about the liberation of language, about words loosed from their context, about poetry. (In a passage I really like, he writes that the pilots of these skybikes "use dust devils as the lift of last resort. You kamikaze into them, treetop high, and hope to rise enough to catch a big convection cell . . . too big, you dement into a winged blue Popsicle.") In this context Santos reminds me of the French utopian Charles Fourier, and both men are closer to the *furor poeticus* of Plato than they are to a hard-minded historian like Marx or a more sober utopian like Robert Owen. Fourier believed the world would eventually contain thirty-seven million poets equal to Homer, thirty-seven million mathematicians equal to Newton, and thirty-seven million dramatists equal to Molière—although, he admitted, these were only "approximate estimates." He believed there were 810 psychological types and organized his *phalanstères* to include two of each. He believed in nearly complete sexual liberation—sadism, masochism, sodomy, homosexuality, pederasty, bestiality, fetishism, and sex between close relatives—and he also believed that salt would one day leech from the seas and that those seas would in turn become oceans of lemonade.

Some of what Santos is up to might be called Art Brut, although in its American form, as Outsider Art, its

appreciation contains a quotient of irony and class snobbery or condescension that has always bothered me. Plus,
Santos doesn't strictly qualify—too much training, as a
sculptor and muralist, and too much savvy, too much
awareness of his renegade role in relation to the gallery
world. He's something of a pisser, resistant to art rather
than naïvely unaware of its trends, so perhaps the uppercase label that suits him best is Marginal Art. At any
rate, Biosquat has some of the Art Brut stuff—its materials are humble, it's the work of a solitary devoted soul,
it's eccentric and enigmatic, it's being undertaken in near
total disregard of public opinion—and one day it may
resemble the Watts Towers or the Palais Idéal. Biosquat
is packed with thought, text-like, and its themes—cy-
cling, nomadism, trash worship, solar power—touch
everything from the fences to the toilets. The toilet I
used, for instance, is your traditional white porcelain
seat mounted on a trike, and when you're done, you toss
in some mulch (not lime, which, Santos says, just turns
the waste into a bunch of brick turds), and then periodically the whole contraption is inched forward, leaving in
its trail a swath of fertilizer suitable for gardening. In a
couple places around the property there were also pissoirs
fashioned out of plastic Clorox bottles, from which the
bottoms had been snipped, and black hoses that then
ran into beds of wood chips, the exact agro-purpose of

which escaped me, but had something to do, I imagine, with urine's nitrogen content. The emunctory enthusiasms of people in eco-villages, always fiddling with their waste, might make for an interesting study, but meanwhile the tricycle toilet at Biosquat worked wonderfully. It didn't stink at all, a claim I'd seriously doubted when Dave Santos first mentioned it, and crapping alfresco is always nice.

One of the laws of Biosquat, it seemed, was that nothing could be what it was originally. The gnat goggles were made from the screens of a tea infuser; to the fat ends of a set of chopsticks Santos had fixed, on one, a tablespoon, and on the other, a toothbrush. He called this general category of transformation "mutant technology." Some of these transformations—especially the bikes—are right in the grain of a particular brand of American genius that flourished in the years following World War II. This genius centered around car culture, and the era probably reached its meridian in Southern California, in the fifties and sixties, waning somewhat by the 1970s. Dave Santos isn't all that different in spirit from a SoCal gearhead like Ed "Big Daddy" Roth, automotive designer and visionary, creator of Rat Fink, who pioneered the use of fiberglass in car bodies and was a guru/hero to the legions of boys who built scale models of his hot rods—the Outlaw, the Beatnik

Bandit, the Mysterion—and any shade-tree mechanic who had an aesthetic bone aching in his body. Roth was celebrated in Tom Wolfe's seminal early essay "The Kandy-Kolored Tangerine-Flake Streamline Baby," and even today his legacy of transformed, souped-up, mutant machines hasn't entirely gone away. The idea of an utterly reworked kick-ass car is still amply evident among the Hispanic boys who cruise Hollywood Boulevard on Friday nights, although in the main that lexicon has gone out of the life of white kids (those who don't live in Barstow or Bakersfield or Stockton, anyway).

Now auto shop's dead, and probably hipsters study art, anyway, but back in the day a certain, perhaps limited manhood made its way into public by lovingly (and literally) deconstructing one of the culture's main givens—the car—and metamorphosing it with saws and torches, complex paints and layers of lacquer, until it shed its dull utility and became art—primarily, as Wolfe says, sculpture. (Roth cast the bodies of his bizarro cars with plaster molds.) It's no accident that this kind of revamping flourishes in macho cultures, since it's so openly about the male need of outlets for sensitivity that aren't permissible and are, in fact, studiously removed from spectacles like football. In an essay quite similar in gist to Wolfe's, Dave Hickey argues that hot-rodding is about dissent, which I think is partially true. Hispanics in LA, for example, often favor hopped-up trucks, in part to recoup and then triumph over the denigrations of migrant labor life, spent riding around dusty fields, packed in the backs of pickups like loads of produce. The very qualities that make a truck functional for farmwork—beefy suspension, extra clearance, etc.—are completely subverted in a lowrider, which couldn't handle even the slightest rut without high-centering or fatally bashing the rocker panels. Lowriders are so outrageously spiffy and cool—a new dandyism—they look like they've never done a day of work in their lives.

And just so, Dave Santos's bikes are ridiculous from the standpoint of utility. Everything an elite rider might want for the Tour de France—lightness, strength, balance, low resistance—is out the window once Santos fires up his torch and begins to build a mutant bike for his migratory trips to Mexico: lengthening the seat tubes by a couple of feet, raising the bottom brackets, setting the chain rings and cranks on a vertical axis, chopping the forks, making the saddles cushy with wads of foam and a wrap of duct tape, improvising fairings of plaster and fabric. They aren't conventionally beautiful, these bikes, and they don't even seem roadworthy—they're circus bikes for goofy, toppling clowns—but in their strange, abstracted state they're definitely objects, maybe sculptures. Everything Dave Santos does at Biosquat is an attempt to render a vivid interior external, and as such, his bikes are primarily an index to the visionary mind of the maker. But the central problem with any visionary experience, plaguing all seers, is one of verification. I'm not talking about vision as an eyeball thing (*Did you see that?*), but vision as imagination, intuition, revelation (*Did you experience that?*), where issues of authenticity, truth, and validity (*Are you nuts?*) become hugely problematic—for example, when you're talking about winged bikes, fitted with feathers of old, still utile trash, that might one day carry hippies to the stratosphere.

At one point Santos said he was fascinated by "those little golden ages that are gone before you know it." But he also said: "That's where I'm a little pessimistic, because sometimes cultures reach a peak and they don't just keep on going forever, you know—then there's ruins, and thousands of years, and, you know, after ancient Greece, they had a lot of downtime, the action went somewhere else. So there's a lot of sadness, a lot of missed opportunities, a lot of mistakes." Biosquat aspires to get outside this story. It's an attempt at creating some kind of suspension, anyway—a world of signs and wonders, of marvels and revelations, of continuous amazement. How? Every object at Biosquat is tinkered with until it's an original, toyed with until it resembles nothing else. Even Santos's fondness for neologisms is a way of wrenching old words into something new and unique. I'd never seen a toothbrush on a chopstick—it's so Dada and sensible at the same time—nor had I taken a shit on a trike. Each object—like Big Daddy Roth's hot rods or the Hispanic boys' chopped and channeled trucks—is an attempt to seize life at a moment of glory, to embody an essence and hold it, stilling the ephemeral, apotheosizing what would otherwise pass, as all things pass. The mutant bikes, the bamboo beds, the gnat goggles and the Chicano robots and the corrugated plastic domes are all singular—freaky, a one-off, an aberrance, a whole world of exceptions. All of it exists somewhere beyond sadness or mistakes or missed opportunities, because, transformed, there's nothing to compare it to. It's meant to speak to you in the language of the burning bush, it's supposed to be a walk on water, it's all truth of another order, as William James says, like the coin Christ pulls from the mouth of the fish to pay the temple tax. These are called miracles, of course, and they break a lot of natural laws, but as transformations, utterly singular, beyond argument, they too are meant to convince you that the kingdom has already arrived, here on Earth. ❖

Orphans

The intent of a façade is exoteric but there are obvious
problems with that. While in St. Petersburg, for instance, I stayed for several days at the Moscow Hotel.
That particular exterior does the work of a façade, presenting a warren of windows so relentlessly uniform the
eye is baffled and ultimately rejected; from a distance,
you can't quite locate the entrance. But if, from outside,
you can't find a way in, from inside, especially walking
the hallways, you can't imagine a way out. The interior
space is made of incredibly long, horrid corridors lined
on either side with black doors, like answers to a question you'd long ago forgotten. You feel exhausted, seeing
such a dreary path ahead of you on the way to your
room. You begin to feel the life behind any one of the

black doors will do—any future, any destiny. Once inside, your room, it turns out, is only the imitation of something nice, an arrangement of resemblances.

And probably the most esoteric Russian encounter is with a woman seated inside a glass booth. You look through thick Plexiglas, you speak into a small vent or round hole, and the grim interior light from a low-watt lamp, the dull brown walls, the sense of the woman as someone seated at the bottom of a box, all of this seems to encourage her indifference, embolden it. Everything inside—the adding machine or cash register, the telephone, the woman's lips—looks antiquated. You may want to exchange money or call a cab or simply make an inquiry, but you are clearly intruding on an isolation that's sanctioned or bolstered, somehow, by an official boredom. What sense of desire or anticipation can you expect from a woman locked away like this, limited to such a small immobilizing space? It seems to be a matter of perfect indifference whether or not you have rubles to spend or the question you want to ask is ever answered. It's like tricking a troll, hoping for passage. If you can consider a façade the blank face, then the woman inside the glass booth is the hardened heart, neither of them inclined to charm. Their efficacy comes from elsewhere. You can't imagine the liberation of such a woman, from either her booth or her boredom, and the information you're after is isolated too, like a dwindling, rationed commodity, lacking market efficiency and flow. In my limited experience, you never came away from one of these occult encounters with enough of what you were after. The arrangement is tightfisted, as though ideas and information weren't meant to circulate, as if they could actually be contained inside what amounted to aquariums. You look into that glass booth long enough and what you begin to see, I imagine, is your own soul.

Or whatever—but I'd felt somewhat pixilated from the moment I stepped off the plane in St. Petersburg. The international airport there's no better than an American bus station, small, dingy, bleak, with that strange lassitude that seems almost the opposite of travel, as if no one's really going anywhere. Somebody was supposed to meet me, and I lingered around this dreary green lobby, reading and rereading the placards people were holding up, but none of the signs had my name written on it. It occurred to me I might call the woman who was supposed to pick me up. In my pocket I had just a crumpled dollar. I talked to one woman in a glass booth who couldn't tell me how to use the phone, and another, obviously distressed woman, also in a glass booth—the information booth—who was hiding beneath a shelf and would not raise her head up and talk to anyone, let alone explain to me how to use the phone. I kept walking over to the wall where the telephone was mounted and staring at it. It looked exactly like a phone but it might as well have been a confounding objet d'art. I went outside and sat. The air was gritty with particulate matter, dust blown in from the barren fields surrounding the runways. It was hard to tell if the airport was under construction or being dismantled. Pieces of metal sheathing flapped in the wind, and the fences meant to cordon the work areas were falling down. A sign gave "apologies for the inconveniences connected with terminal reconstruction." Back inside I found yet another woman in yet another glass booth who sold phone cards. Eventually, outside, I managed to make a phone work and I called my contact, who said she was so sorry, she thought I was arriving tomorrow, but for roughly 1,500 rubles I could easily catch a cab to the Moscow Hotel.

More than money what I needed was rest, at the very least to quell the misgivings I had been having about my role as a writer. On the transatlantic leg of the flight I had sketched out a bunch of alternatives: I mulled over writing in the urgent voice of a liberal reformer, or expressing a stoic world-weariness, or getting riled up and angry in an exposé, or working toward a generous-spirited puff piece. These were all stories I thought about telling. And then on the plane from Frankfurt to St. Petersburg I was fated to sit beside a couple from Cleveland who were coming to Russia to adopt an eight-year-old girl. The girl, they told me, had been abandoned by her family, which the man attributed to the shift from a "communistic to a capitalistic society." He said this quite emphatically. In fact he was an emphatic person the way other people are tenors or baritones, and because I had the window seat and felt trapped I began to get buggy. Everything he said stuck to my skin. He asked a lot of questions that were aggressive and blunt and designed to elicit or provoke simple yes or no answers. It wasn't a conversation; he was just beating the air like a rug, hoping to knock all the doubt and ambiguity out of it. I kept wondering—strangely—if he was an *avocat*; I mean I wondered if he was a lawyer, using the French word in my head. All three hours of the flight I felt like I'd been locked away in an interrogation room.

His wife seemed kind and sweet and obsequious, with a soft chin that marred her real chance at beauty. Every time I looked at her face I felt lost. She had that bright-eyed, very dull niceness well-meaning people often have that strikes you as full of shit until you realize there's nothing behind it. It's real. She was nice. When she asked about my business in Russia I was totally incoherent, and once her husband, the avocat, sniffed me out, he really started hammering the air with questions. Now I was on trial. I became almost spastically inarticulate and confused and couldn't describe what I was doing in a satisfactory narrative style. By the time we landed, my business had become a shame to me, a fault of mine; I was guilty. They, on the other hand, had a story whose somewhat gooey mucilage was goodness, this couple from Cleveland. I'd just read about this very thing on the plane from Chicago to Frankfurt, poring over a learned article on attachment disorders and the developing mind— my sister thought it might be relevant in observing orphans—in which the author talked about some guy named Grice and his four maxims of discourse:

1. Quality: be truthful and have evidence for what you say.
2. Quantity: be succinct.
3. Relation: be relevant or perspicacious, presenting what has to be said so that it is plainly understood.
4. Manner: be clear and orderly.

Supposedly violating any one of these precepts indicates mental problems, and I'd just hashed all of them.

But the couple from Cleveland were like Grice apostles. That's why they were adopting a child: they had a story in mind.

It was with a feeling of relief, then, that I made it out of St. Petersburg, five hours by two-lane road, to Svirstroy. At the orphanage, bare-limbed birch trees lined the driveway leading to the front door. Snow was still on the ground, patches of snow drifted into the protecting shade of pine trees, even though at this time of year, in May, the sun wasn't setting until after eleven o'clock at night.

Within an hour of my arrival a couple different kids, independently, asked when I was leaving. It seemed a strange question, out of sequence, but the defining fact of these kids' lives, I would realize, is the transience of adults. A lovely, soulfully sweet girl named Tonia told me her history in epochal blocks marked by the passage of adults, like a dry account of royal succession. Up till seven she lived with her mother and father, from eight to nine she lived with either friends or her aunt, from nine to eleven she lived with her grandmother, who died of stomach cancer on August 19, 1995—the way Tonia mentioned the exact date seemed salient in a life lived largely without celebrated days. Anyway, deep down there must have been huge anxiety about departures, and the question, I came to understand, was meant to allay a real fear about the fragility of adult relations. What the kids wanted to know was how much of their interest they should invest in me, another ghostly passing adult—in other words, what's the rate of return on caring?

A boy named Kosta bluntly told me I wasn't staying long enough to write anything, and when I asked how long he thought I needed, he said three months, a year. He wasn't being cutting or cruel or defensive, just thinking about and weighing the world, his world, after all. One afternoon I went to the village and bought hot dogs and bread, ketchup and mustard, pop and cookies, and about fifteen of us lit a big bonfire on the banks of the river and had a picnic. By the way, none of these kids goldbrick or grouse when it comes to work. They have chores at the orphanage, and when it came time to gather wood for our fire, suddenly and without a second prompting it was madness—they hopped to, hauling branches and logs and sticks and armloads of dry grass, and we had our fire blazed up in minutes. But after we'd eaten and were lazing around, watching big ships haul raw logs upriver, a beautiful boy, Maxim, smiled and said, "That was good food, but it's over. Write it down. Write it down in the magazine." The comment stuck with me. Like everyone I tend to think things that last have greater value than passing moments, and on some level, too, I was probably condescending to the kids. I thought I was treating them to something they'd not soon forget. On both counts Maxim, in a frank, simple, cynical way, was putting things in perspective for me—his perspective.

The orphanage was built originally as housing for pilots in training, and for several years after World War II it held German and Hungarian prisoners, some of whom, across an open field, are buried and memorialized in a grove of trees. A couple years ago some old people came, the kids told me, and cried. This seemed to mystify them, how people would remember each other, and especially the dead, over such a vast stretch of time. You imagine, of course, that the prisoners buried behind the orphanage perhaps left orphans themselves, and that these old people, on a final pilgrimage, might well have been visiting their fathers. The kids' comments captured a certain—I won't say blockage—but a dreamy remove from a reality that would be fairly pedestrian for most people. It would not be the last time I noticed this sort of loose drift in their associations, an ellipsis in the mind that helped them slide over rough terrain in their history.

At the edge of the orphanage property are what the kids call the red ruins and the black ruins, and I was taken on a tour of both, each interior with the same dust, the same broken slant of light, the same weeds and rubble and cracked glass, but the black ruin is a former bomb shelter dug deep into the ground, and the red ruin, a brick building above ground, seems once to have housed a repair shop of some sort—there were steel doors of outsized proportions meant to allow the passage of trucks. In the red ruin padlocks remained on doors without hinges, and wire bars gated windows without glass. The ruins mainly suggest a kind of contrapuntal relation to the orphanage itself, which dates from the same era yet still stands. In America, looking back, we don't really arrive at history so much as we enter romance, some place of eternal beginnings, but here, even in the bucolic Russian countryside, the devastations of war are marked by dead prisoners, shelters, stone defilades and, deep in the woods, what I took to be bomb craters—suspiciously odd declivities in an otherwise smoothly rolling or flat landscape. Here, there are ruins, and then there are things saved from ruin, things that escape, and the difference is emphatically alive and real, even if you can't calculate why by using the ungovernable terms of historical destiny.

Maybe more than the building itself, the land around the orphanage and the elaborate network of footpaths create for the kids a sense of place. There are trails through the birch and pine, across fields where, every spring, the kids burn leaves and work the ash into the soil and plant potatoes, trails that lead to the river, to the school, to the village, to ponds and creeks and springs flowing up from beneath the ground with cool, drinkable water, trails that are a story in themselves, worn by wandering feet over fifty years, worn by joy and hope and habit and need, trails like a sentence spoken, each a whisper about the surrounding world, a dialogue with doubt or desire that's ultimately answered by a destination. Many of the children have either no history or a severely foreshortened sense of the past, but these trails, worked into the grass or through the forests by others before them, send the kids off to play in a shared world—shared not just in physical space, but down through time. It must in some humble way ease the isolation, like Crusoe finding a footprint in the sand.

Time and a lot of touching have turned the interior of the orphanage funky, with a lived-in feel that now will likely never go away—it's there in the worn wood, the marble steps chipped or cracked so long ago that the original sharp, jagged wounds have since been smoothed and cicatrized like a weal by countless passing feet. The paint on the railings is layers thick, the broken windows are patched but not replaced, the tiles that peel up remain missing. Things inside were so worn and rubbed and handled by living beings that the interior had lost a lot of its rectangularity, and was replaced, instead, by a roundedness, a kind of inner burrowed shape arrived at by working the materials from within, like the nest of a wren. I found this fascinating, and loved discovering touches of it, combing the place for evidence of the tide of children, the softening action of them against the hard surfaces and correct angles favored by the original architects. Doorsills were scooped like shells by scuffling kids, and the jambs, at various heights, had lost their edge as lingering children held them, dirtied them, and picked at them until they had to be repainted, over the years, with many quick coats of high-gloss enamel. The stone floors held smooth undulations where the kids habitually walked, wearing troughs that you could feel by skimming your feet across them, and that you could see, in certain lights, as a rippling reflection. Heavily trafficked areas of the orphanage received the most paint, so the lower walls had a receptive, accepting density, an imperfect but pliant look, and the railings on the stairwells, though made of metal, looked like they'd been recently dipped in hot caramel.

The kids live in spacious, decent rooms with high ceilings and big windows. The boys pasted stuff to the walls—ads for cars torn from magazines or pictures of German rock stars ripped from the newspaper—and scrawled a little graffiti with black felt pens—in other words, pretty much a rendition of a boy's room in America, but without the wherewithal. In one of the rooms, a hole had been punched in the wall, through the plaster and lath, which the boys used to communicate with the kids in the adjoining room. That it was unsightly didn't bother them one bit. They called it their telephone. These same boys later showed me their pet rats, and at the base of a plywood divider meant to keep males and females separate, the rats, too, had begun to gnaw a hole into the next room. I can't wring a dark poignancy out of the comparison between rats and orphan boys, however, because Svirstroy just wasn't that way. What the boys did wasn't vandalism, it wasn't destructive or ornery. If anything, the hole in the wall was a rough, clumsy modification the kids made because they're extremely close to one another. They'd restructured the building to suit their needs; that hole in the wall was about their hope for love. It may have looked destructive, but it was really an act of restoration. In general, boys and girls alike sought each other out, they sought and found proximity, and no one seemed at all defensive about their space. This seeking was one of the more noticeable aspects of my stay there. Relaxing on the lawn or sitting by the river, the kids would naturally clump up, pillowing their heads against each others' bellies, a whole chain of children in a circle, all quite free and unguarded about touching.

In an American institution the general disrepair might be seen as signs of decrepitude and disintegration, of a shoddy slide, but the direction at the orphanage seemed quite the opposite, upward, integral, a sense of pieces coming together. The clinical rectitude that serves us so well in America might also prevent us from doing the human thing in some cases, and I can't quite imagine an old building, owned by the government, turned over to the care and maintenance of kids; the impulse would probably be quashed by the obstacles. We'd have to knock Svirstroy down and haul it away in pieces before we could begin. In an obliquely related theme, my whole time at the orphanage I could never find any wastebaskets; my pockets filled with trash. In America of course every public hallway has a rich battery of waste-disposal options, with separate receptacles for newsprint, pop cans, apple cores, or whatever. For obvious reasons, poor orphan kids don't generate much garbage. Generally, their present doesn't obsolesce and convert into the past quite as rapidly as it does for kids in America; there isn't the abundance, and in the absence of a steady stream of the new, stuff doesn't get used up and sloughed so easily. (The boys, for instance, hoarded batteries for their Walkmans, and deftly rewound cassettes by manually whirling the sprockets with hexagonal Bic pens to conserve power.) The building itself was testimony to this kind of make-do endurance. We'd see in a place like Svirstroy an affront to newness, which in America is the path to the future, and our sensibility might prove problematic, on the level of some aesthetic or metaphoric blockage, in kicking off a project like an orphanage. We'd wonder how you could hope to offer children a future in a building so evidently scarred by the past.

The very best night I spent at the orphanage was with a young woman named Yana. She was sixteen and lived with four other girls, dorm-style, in a room she'd occupied for the past nine years. You could feel the resonance her long tenure brought to the space. She'd obviously lavished love on it, which in turn probably set the tone for the other girls. The economy of love in the orphanage seemed to work that way—it was passed quite efficiently from one kid to the next. Love spread horizontally, across the broad, extended present of the orphanage; it wasn't invested in a future or sequestered in a solitary, longed-for past. The beds were neatly, uniformly made, with pleasant colorful quilts and matching pillowcases, and Yana had strung a philodendron on monofilament so that, trained, its healthy green cordate leaves circled the room airily overhead, like a string of unripe hearts. On the walls were glitzy pictures of Britney Spears, Christina Aguilera, etc. At one point Yana got up, peeled back the corner of a poster, and showed the cracked plaster beneath; she'd put the pictures there to cover what she called "the bad places." She was a little shy about it, shy as if the damaged plaster reflected on her personally, but she also seemed proud of the improvements she'd made. She had rodents, like the boys, but these were cute, cuddly mice, a boy and a girl, and she kept them in a large jar of soft, fine wood shavings and, with no divider, planned to share the eventual offspring with other kids in the orphanage.

Yana had been at Svirstroy for eleven years. She said she had no idea where her mother and father were, but presumably they were somewhere, alive; an uncle, alcoholic, last paid her a visit eight years ago.

She asked if I'd like to see her photo album, and when I said I would, the room suddenly got very quiet. And then her shier roommates, encouraged, brought out their albums. It's hard to imagine or adequately describe what an album of photographs might mean to an orphaned girl of sixteen. One thing that was immediately apparent was that Yana herself did not own a camera.

The pictures in her possession were taken by others, by visiting Americans, by one or two kids who'd been adopted and then sent back snapshots of themselves in Disneyland, by representatives of the various charitable organizations that come through a couple times a year. In other words, they were copies of photographs taken, most centrally, as an event in someone else's life. Yana herself was a touristic stop in somebody's trip to Russia. In every single shot she was posed; there were no candid moments, no moments outside the fragilely constructed instant. Naturally, the pictures didn't serve a nostalgic function. They hardly offered a chronology, capturing, instead, the present tense of life at Svirstroy. The scenery surrounding Yana never changed radically; the orphanage was her constant backdrop. Judging by the album alone, Yana was never a baby, she was never a toddler taking a first step, she was never a communicant in white lace walking up the aisle at church, she'd never had a birthday or ridden a bike—and so on and on and on. In a way, family photographs are a record of the parents' watchful eyes, a chart of the unfolding future they've planned and invested in, but a sense of that forward-looking scrutiny was entirely absent in her album. These photographs were taken by strangers, and some of that exchange, the character of it, remained in every picture, in the posed quality, the drifting gaze, the blank or baffled or forced expression. In a regular family album, the kids grow, their bodies change, and that's largely what's being documented; and half the time the true subject is in the background, it's about a day at the beach, it's about the snow in the mountains, it's about the garden in back of grandma's house—it's about the children as they exist in the world. But in Yana's album there was no such verification. She existed, solely, at the orphanage.

When I asked the kids if they were happy, none of them could really answer; the question, I gathered, was puzzling. "Happiness is a big word," Tonia told me, after a long, stalled silence. Then, through the translator, of course, she said she was happiest when there was understanding, when "things go good for others," when people love each other. I realized then that I was asking a typically American question about the state or sovereignty of the self. It was a question that assumed a primary and absolute right to an interior self, and she, like so many of the kids, looked instead to the outer world, the world of contact, of presence. Eventually, she did say one of her best memories was when the other kids surprised her with a gift and a cake and lemonade at a birthday party she wasn't expecting. What seemed to move Tonia was that they'd "prepared ahead," that she'd been held in mind by others, remembered for a duration, and given a passing sense of what a future, filled with loving concern, might feel like. And that's the way it was at Svirstroy. None of the kids expressed a sense of being rooked out of an imagined rightful life, and if perhaps, darkly, they'd developed minds and equipped their souls with buffers so pain was not cumulative and the present tense of experience neither stemmed from the past nor was predicated on a future, so be it. They were home.

One day I was led through the woods by ten or so kids until we came to a spring that emerged from the base of a hummock marked by a large Russian Orthodox cross. A small wooden platform had been placed beside the spring, to stand on as you fetched water; next to it was a forked stick, like a coatrack, dangling with drinking cups someone had made by cutting plastic bottles in half. We all drank, and the water was cool and clean, it felt like water should feel, holy, a moment where time stops, and the quenching of thirst, on that day as on any really good day in your life, was as much a matter of communion as breaking bread or sharing wine. In some simple way this was the site of a special meaning, and the kids had led me, like an acolyte, to a place where I could drink and refresh myself in a communal mystery. Svirstroy was a place where love circulated, and somehow what's good there was registering in me. I was feeling it. I'm sure I was. These children never showed self-pity, and if anything they'd taken the hollow where that emotion normally settles and filled it with each other. In fairy tales every juncture along the trail, no matter how dark or forbidding, is met with a yes, and that's how they unfold and why, deep down, they soothe our fears. Here, inside the shared present, was the happiness Tonia was talking about.

It's natural enough to hope tomorrow will cure today, and the core of the problem, of futures that recoup current difficulties, cropped up again when the translator brought to my attention the business of money: his $200, the orphanage's $150, the driver's $300, the hotel's $200, none of which I had. I was dead broke. I'd traveled halfway around the world with a dollar in my left pocket that was more talisman or trinket than anything else. I'd been boldly approached by a lovely Russian hooker in the lobby of the Moscow Hotel, a beautiful blonde with Heidi braids and endearing broken English and a Russian-novel name, Katarina, all very tempting, but that transaction, like everything else, was beyond my means. She refused to believe I was broke. We argued about it! She wanted to know how much money I made "every month in America." I felt like we were trying to negotiate a swap of cultural clichés. I was too embarrassed to tell her that basically my mother and sister and brother-in-law had been supporting me until my new mood stabilizers kicked in and I could once again think clearly about my life, i.e., get out of bed in the morning. For the kids at Svirstroy, the circulation of money, Russian or otherwise, was never an issue. Most of the boys beyond the age of ten smoke, and cigarettes, for them, act as a kind of coin, a wealth to be acquired and traded and shared. The absence of "real" money, flat money, is essentially the absence of a future. Not that the boys lack one—rather, possible futures never enter into their calculations; a cigarette equals pleasure, not the hoarding of deferred possibilities. In America, the sight of little boys with cigarettes would be shocking, but I have to say these guys were kind of cute, in a Little Rascally way, puffing smokes in their sloppy orphan clothes.

The other currency we traded in was words. None of the kids spoke English, although one boy I really liked a lot, Sasha, would say, "Good morning. I'm glad to see you." And other kids liked floating the few words they knew my way. They traded these words like chits in a game about relationships: Limp Bizkit, hip-hop, Linkin Park, etc. Language probably always has this adhesive aspect, but it's more noticeable when you struggle for words, when you constantly skirt the edges of failure.

When I was on my own, alone with the kids, they either shouted in Russian, as if I were merely dense, or worked with gestures, as though playing charades. The translator was meant to bridge the gap, and he was excellent, keeping the conversation alive to the point that, after a few days, the kids began to realize that I could, on occasion, be pretty funny, and I, in turn, was just beginning to recognize the soulful texture, the nap of personality, in some of the boys and girls I spent the most time with. On the upside, perhaps, our lack of shared language had a filtering effect—rather like a lack of money—giving the past a shallowness, the future a vagueness, and keeping us in an essential present. Paradoxically, translation and the stripping of verb tenses forced us to live together in a physical, shared world. We enjoyed the fresh air, the river, the smell of pine trees. We played games that didn't require talk, and we walked the trails and pathways, letting those old sentences in the forests surrounding Svirstroy speak. Still, working through a translator was hard. Everything came close to a gloss or a paraphrase, losing some degree of nuance, so that it was very difficult to know who was quick-witted or sullen or sensitive, which kids were bright and which were slow. There were questions I didn't ask, particularities and depths I avoided. This failure on the level of fine distinction tends to make you see the kids as a conglomerate, which points the way toward pity, opening you up to a vague and general sadness at exactly the moment when, because you'll never have to do anything particular, it's safe.

One little thing I saw over and over again filled me with a low-grade despair and a lingering, elusive sadness I could never quite identify. Even now I can approach it only roundaboutly.

A lot of things the kids were into had a definite prison character. I don't mean the kids were criminal or delinquent, not by a long shot, but there was a sense of damaged or boxed-up futurity, similar in feature, though less extreme, to convicts. A book of matches had a fairly high valuation, as did cigarettes, stickers, and hair clips, which was more the sign of an underlying scarcity and an uncertain future than a reflection of real cost. These things were squeezed for every remaining ounce of meaning. Some of the boys held on to dead batteries, for instance, collecting them for their trinket value long after they'd lost their utility. Hair clips and cigarettes are known as commodity money, money with intrinsic value, which is close kin to barter and, at this point, at least in modern societies, a very distant relation to fiat money, which has no intrinsic value. The few times I saw the kids with cash, the bills actually looked more like a strange text than a token of value. If flat money speaks to the future or, through debt, keeps up a conversation with the past, then barter addresses the present—it's all about right now. Being broke can make for a kind of immediacy, and so can bartering, if being exposed to vicissitudes, quite nakedly, without defense, is the measure; whereas flat money and fluid markets free us up from time and space, the local insults of the seasons, the impoverishment of the soil beneath our feet, etc. But when the future suffers a disturbance, as it does for an orphaned child or prisoner, or as it often does in war, money either tends toward barter or finds more fluidity by going underground. About Warsaw during World War II, Czesław Miłosz says: "Life, as for primitive man, once more depended on the seasons of the year. Autumn was the hardest because potatoes and coal had to be gotten for the long, hopeless winter."

The curious tension here is that children are the future, and the ruptured promise a place like Svirstroy tries to repair is vast. The future requires kids; without them, there's eventually no tomorrow. In time, of course, everybody runs out of tomorrows. The one thing you can say about the future, Joseph Brodsky has written, is that it won't include you. That's true, and yet the dyad of money and children plots you way out there in that world of tomorrows you don't get. Your dream, then, is of a nothingness where an investment of love lives on. You believe in a time that's not your own. The main problem with barter is the need for a coincidence of wants: you have to want what the other person's got, and vice versa. And you have to arrive at a specific place in the universe on time. And here's the thing that was so hard for me to feel precisely: over and over, what I saw at Svirstroy were these little hands passing things, bottle caps and cigarettes, a cookie, a twig or leaf, small frequent exchanges where skin contacted skin, just briefly, but perfectly timed, now. In the enormity of their dislocation, the kids arrived for each other, always. They were there, they were present, and bartering was the deal that confirmed it. It made me sad, these transactions, these little dirty hands reaching and finding, this coincidence of wants, taking place inside a huge broken promise. Born into a world where their wants went unmet, where their time was taken away, they found reassuring coincidence in bartering. In those little moments I felt like I was seeing the kids isolated—lovingly so—in currents that were crushing them.

But let's say, since it's natural enough, that tomorrow really is a remedy for today. Back in St. Petersburg there was still the heavily pending matter of money. The translator came to the Moscow Hotel on Saturday, ostensibly to arrange for a transfer of funds and then take me to a public market, where I hoped to pick up a few souvenirs. Plus I wanted to return his abundant kindness by treating him to a nice dinner. The good people at *Nest* magazine had wired cash, and I was relieved, even feeling magnanimous, like a regular, upright, solvent citizen. The translator handed me a receipt, and I noticed all the agreed-upon prices had been jacked up by thirty dollars, like a customs or tariff on my confusion. He called the bank but the phone just rang and rang. Then he said we'd take a cab to the bank, as if that were a reasonable assumption to draw from an unanswered phone. Myself, I pictured an empty, dark room, but the translator must have imagined something else; what, I don't know. We caught a jitney cab, just some beat guy driving around in a Lada, and for a hundred rubles, roughly three dollars, he drove us way the hell out past a ghetto of gray Soviet housing, into a flat wasteland reclaimed from swamp sometime in the eighteenth century. Three hundred years later the swamp seemed to be rising, phoenixlike, in the form of pale white dust. The roads were fucked—islands of level pavement surrounded by deep holes. All our business—cab fare, directions, destination—was being conducted in Russian, of course, so when we arrived at a sprawling compound fenced and topped with razor wire, the mystery had a gentle logic that even the uniformed guards, with machine guns slung over their shoulders, couldn't dispel, not entirely. The Russians had seemed weird about money and market efficiency, and perhaps guys with guns made more sense in the former Republic than a row of tellers. The translator looked at the place and said, "Strange."

We finally found the building, found the room number, and knocked on the door, even though it was slightly ajar in a very un-bank-like manner. There was no one inside. The room didn't even remotely resemble a bank, although perhaps interior space needs a translator as much as language does. The translator talked at length with a woman across the hall, who'd been sitting, alone, in a nearly identical room, reading a paperback novel, and who insisted there was no bank in the compound. We quickly flagged down another crappy Lada and rode a completely different way back to the Moscow Hotel and made more phone calls in pursuit of the money. It all felt like a shell game, and, anyway, I wanted to hurry out and buy a chess set for my niece and maybe visit Anna Akhmatova's last residence, now a museum. I was hoping to hang out at Dostoevsky's tomb too, especially since old Fyodor, beset by gambling debts most of his life, was starting to seem like the patron saint of my trip. However, it seemed unlikely that the translator, disappointed about the money, was going to take me to any markets or show me the way to some old poet's house, and ultimately he just left me on my own and said good-bye. He'd lost his interest in me. Maybe he was broke too.

Back at the orphanage, a day earlier, one of the kids, Ruslan, had asked me a riddle. There's a donkey, he said, trapped on an island in the middle of the ocean. A volcano is erupting on the island and rivers of hot lava are flowing toward the donkey. In addition, all around the small island is a ring of fire. What, Ruslan wanted to know, would you do? I thought about it, came up blank, and said I didn't know. And Ruslan, with a smile, said: the donkey didn't know either. ❖

PART 3:
READING LIFE

Teach: Without this we're just savage shitheads in the wilderness.

Don: Yeah.

Teach: Sitting around some vicious campfire.

—DAVID MAMET, *American Buffalo*

Salinger and Sobs

In the days immediately after my brother killed himself
I'd go into the backyard and lie on our picnic table and
watch the November wind bend the branches of a tall
fir tree across the street. Really hard gusts would shake
loose a raucous band of black crows and send them
wheeling into the sky. They'd caw and cackle and circle
and resettle and rise again, crowing, I guess, a noisy
mocking counterpart to the flock of strangers in funer-
ary black who'd shown up to bury my brother. About
a week after Danny'd put a gun to his head and pulled
the trigger and a couple days after his lame orthodox
funeral at our childhood church, I went for a walk
along a street of patched potholes that runs around
Lake Union (near where, a year or so into the future, a

future I was sure had ended tragically the night Danny shot himself, my other brother Mike would pull a similar stunt, jumping off the Aurora Bridge and living to tell about it, thus revealing to me the comic, the vaudevillian underside of suicide) and saw a scavenging crow jabbing its beak into the breast of an injured robin. The robin had probably first been hit by a car. It was flipped on its back and badly maimed, but it wasn't carrion quite yet. One wing was pinned to its breast and the other flapped furiously in a useless struggle for flight and thus the bird, still fiercely instinctive, only managed to spin around in circles like the arrow you flick with your finger in a game of chance. The robin was fully alive, but it was caught in a futile hope, and I knew this, and the crow knew this, and while the crow taunted the bird, hopping down from its perch on a nearby fence, pecking at the robin, returning to its roost, waiting, dropping down and attacking again, I stood off to the side of the road and watched.

I'll tell you the ultimate outcome of this lopsided contest a little later, but for now I bring it up only because, some years ahead, fully inhabiting my aborted future, I often ask myself a koan-like question re: my brother that goes something like this: If I could intervene and change my own particular history would I alter past events in such a way that I'd bring Danny back to life? Would I return the single rimfire bullet to its quiet chamber in the gun and let the night of November 26, 19__, pass away in sleep and dreams or drink or television or whatever the anonymous bulk of history holds for most people? Would I uncurl the fingers from the grip, would I take away the pain, would I unwrite the note and slip the blank sheet back in the ream and return the ream to pulp and etc., would I exchange my own monstrous father for some kindly sap out of the sitcom tradition, would I do any of this, would I? And where would I be? Would I be there, in the room? Would my role be heroic? And where exactly would I begin digging into the past, making corrections, amending it? How far back do I have to go to undo the whole dark kit and kaboodle? I mean, from where I sit now I can imagine a vast sordid history finally reaching its penultimate unraveled state in the Garden, under the shade of the tree of knowledge, raising the question of whether or not I'd halt the innocent hand, leaving the apple alone, unbitten.

I'm a little wary of prelapsarian schemes in much the same way I'm leery of conspiracy theories, both of which seem only to describe the limitations, like Hamlet's nutshell, of the holder's mind. You don't really want to crash down the whole universe just to satisfy your situational unease or your incapacity to see the whole picture, do you? You don't want a life based on your failure to understand life, right? If I were able to undo Danny's death would that mean, too, that Mike's suicide attempt would never occur, or would it simply mean that he'd find an alternate, more surefire lethality than leaping over the rail of Seattle's most famous suicide spot, a spot that's worked just hunky-dory for hundreds of others? Or would my remaining brother drown or die of internal injuries instead of, as it turned out, smacking the water, breaking his pelvis, destroying his bladder, dislocating his shoulder and yet, that screwed up (plus I forgot to mention his schizophrenia), still having the presence of mind to kick off his boots, swim for shore, pull a quarter out of his pants, and call an ambulance for himself, easy as a man catching a cab? Would that little miracle not happen in this revamped history of mine? Would I just be trading one brother for another? Would I even be writing this, or would a lovely silence reign over my uneventful life, leaving me free to consider other, happier fortunes?

I'd never read J. D. Salinger or John Knowles, both staples of the high school curriculum, because somehow out of the always ripening ambient culture I'd picked up a whiff of the East Coast, of the upper crust and hoity-toity and, ipso facto, at least for me, a kind of irrelevance, irrelevance tinged with a defensive counter-snobbery that's so characteristic of the West. I couldn't identify with the prep-school scene. I thought it was socially atavistic, some stupid idea invented in England. So instead of the boarding-school experiences of Salinger or Knowles I read Joyce's *Portrait of the Artist as a Young Man* strictly for its creepy Jesuit milieu and the way Stephen Dedalus uses difference and snobbery to escape. The reading of *Portrait* was itself a Dedalean act of snobbery on my part, a pose I hoped would piss off the jocks at my Jesuit boys school. Why? Because I *was* a jock, but had recently quit all sports in order to take up managing my misery full-time. At that age, at sixteen, seventeen, I read fiction because I needed advice on how to live, and I needed it to be totally free of judgment. I wanted to see how other people did life. I had exiled myself from the kind of order found on the athletic field, and the alternatives that presented themselves most obviously at my school were to become a dope fiend or a scholar. I tried both and bookishness stuck. By reading I hoped to get as far as I could from Catholic homiletics, and quickly discovered that the best place for moral-free advice was really good fiction. Immediately I saw that stories looked squarely and bravely at lives without criticizing or condemning them. Admittedly, wanting practical advice is a pretty primitive idea of what a book should do, but that's the sort of literary sense I had, treating novels and stories like the self-help manuals that cycle through the decades, reinventing relevance. I didn't know any better, and probably still don't. Anyway, I came late to *The Catcher in the Rye*, as an adult, and thought I'd be somewhat cold to its charms.

I wasn't. Right from the beginning my reading of Salinger's work was lopsided, eccentric, obsessed with the reclusive writer's legendary silence and the theme of suicide that seems to stitch a quilt out of the extant work. As is always, perhaps inevitably the case, the unbalanced weight my own life brought to the material gave the work this off-center, wobbly orbit, and even now I can't seem to read the stuff any differently. It's all about Suicide and Silence. Suicide is first mentioned when Holden, standing on a hill above the football field, says the game with Saxon Hall "was the last game of the year, and you were supposed to commit suicide or something if old Pencey didn't win." Other direct mentions of suicide or thinly veiled threats run through the story. The very word has a casual suggestive presence in Holden's vocabulary. He volunteers to ride on top of the next atomic bomb. And then there's the story he tells of James Castle, the boy who leaps from the window, killing himself, while wearing a black turtleneck he'd borrowed from Holden. It's now generally a given in the literature of suicidology that every attempt is ambivalent, that some degree of chance is worked into each plan, a savior chosen, an opportunity for rescue extended, a tortured hope hidden near the heart of the suicide's rapidly constricting universe. For instance, suicides tend to move *toward* society—and possible intervention—the closer they come to making and carrying out concrete plans. And of course *The Catcher in the Rye* takes its title from precisely this sort of ambivalence, and the story itself, in some ways an extended riff on saving and being saved, is otherwise full of specific strategies for rescue—with Holden nervously alternating point of view, vacillating between rescuer and rescued.

The passage below gives the book its name and is obviously as much about Holden's hope for himself as it is about the fantasy of saving others.

I keep picturing all these little kids playing some game in this big field of rye and all. Thousands of little kids, and nobody's around—nobody big, I mean—except me. And I'm standing on the edge of some crazy cliff. What I have to do, I have to catch everybody if they start to go over the cliff—I mean if they're running and they don't look where they're going I have to come out from somewhere and catch them. That's all I'd do all day. I'd just be the catcher in the rye . . .

I generally don't read biographical gossip about writers, and I don't know a thing, not one scrap, about Salinger's life (other than the silence), but the theme of suicide feels authentic to me, and so does his recurrent big-family thing, two elements I share with—who? Salinger, or his various narrators, or both—or neither? I don't know. Like the Glasses (let's say), we too had seven kids, and one thing that seems to happen in large families more often than in small is that nicknames flourish, partly because there's always some little kid around who can't pronounce the real names of his older siblings. Little kids forming their first syllables corrupt those names, and the corruptions stick because they're cute or funny or whatever. Salinger's Glass family seems to be all nicknames except for Seymour. As the oldest child, I too was somewhat exempt—more namer than named—but a good example of the process from our family would be my sister Patricia, who quickly migrated from "Tricia" to "Trish," and then skipped sideways to "Didya" before finally arriving at "Did." And Did's sisters were Mugs, Gith, and Bean, and Did called my brother Danny "Mr. Sobs," or plain "Sobs," because when they played house he was always the baby. These goofed-up, singsong names recall Franny, Zooey, Boo Boo, etc. And too, in large families, children form their own fairly populous society, separate from the parents, and the nicknames become a kind of argot, a secret language, whereas in small families, I imagine, there's more of an emphasis on vertical and direct contact with the adults. Anyway, Salinger's use of nicknames, the proliferation of them, and the fact that the oldest child, Seymour, doesn't have one, has always been for me an important detail in understanding the work.

In Salinger's work, there is an ongoing failure of the various narrators who occupy center stage, a failure to find a separate and distinct identity outside the corporate idea of family. Holden is a little bit D. B. and Allie and Phoebe, and Buddy is Seymour and Zooey, etc., etc. People from big families tend to have this intense group identity. I don't know why, even though, for instance, I fall easily into the first-person plural when asked about my past. My gut instinct, looking back, is to use "we." Is it size alone that accounts for the blurring of identity in a big family? The fact that you grow up crowded into the same bathroom, brushing your teeth in front of a mirror that has three or four other foamy white grins reflecting back at you—is that it? Or the way you end up wearing some other kid's clothes, or finding a favorite outfit, years after you last wore it, in your brother's drawer, as if he were just another, later edition of you—is that it? Possibly. Privacy, too, is a problem. You rarely get time alone. And with so many competing parties, a constantly negotiated peace accord is necessary if you hope to get along, and for the simplest things, for using a car on Friday night or choosing a channel on the television, you end up working closely, and in concert, with the other kids. In our house, taking this closeness a step farther, we institutionalized the buddy system, a permanent arrangement in which every older kid was assigned a younger, and you were strictly accountable for that child's safety at crosswalks as well as his mischief in the aisles of supermarkets and his happiness during the long wait to buy new play shoes at Penney's. Since I was the oldest, my assigned buddy was my brother Danny, the youngest and rowdiest.

For Salinger's narrators, there's never sufficient separation from the family, at least that sense of family defined horizontally by siblings. Holden really loves only D. B., his dead brother Allie, and his sister Phoebe, mistrusting everyone else. Nobody outside the circle of family seems to make any sense to him, or at least they aren't given the same ample room for oddity he grants his brothers and sisters. Other people simply aren't real to Holden, not in the solid, reassuring way family is. My point here, in discussing identity and family, isn't to draw near a psychological reading of the work. In fact, it seems to me that the decade of the fifties, which saw the first flush of a mass psychological processing of life, right away meets in Holden Caulfield its staunchest resistance. (In *Seymour: An Introduction*, Salinger writes of the psychiatric profession: "They're a peerage of tin ears. With such faulty equipment, with *those* ears, how can anyone possibly trace the pain, by sound and quality alone, back to its source? With such wretched hearing equipment, the best, I think, that can be detected, and perhaps verified, is a few stray, thin overtones—hardly even counterpoint—coming from a troubled childhood or a disordered libido.") There doesn't *seem* to be anything really wrong with Holden, and yet everything is messed up. The conceit of the novel is that Holden's telling the story from inside an institution, and you can imagine, you can hear in the loud nervous prose, that he's making a direct appeal to the reader, going over the heads of doctors and nurses and various experts who don't get it.

The subject of big families might seem fringy but it brings me to the organizing idea of authenticity. It's a central question in all the work. What is real? What is trustworthy? Holden, of course, is famously on guard against phonies, watchful for insincere people or hypocrites, anyone giving a false impression, the pretentious, impostors and perverts. In "A Perfect Day for Bananafish," the trite phone conversation—the false narrative—between the wife and her mother is brutally wrong about Seymour. It's untrue, it says nothing real or accurate about the world. And Buddy Glass, the narrator in *Seymour: An Introduction,* says, "I can usually tell whether a poet or prose writer is drawing from the first-, second-, or tenth-hand experience or is foisting off on us what he'd like to think is pure invention." It's not so much the content of this statement but the very issue of authenticity that piques my interest. The ability to detect authenticity is a critical faculty, something all of us develop, more or less. You can fail on either side, you can be gullible, easily duped, or you can be too skeptical, believing nothing. And with Holden, for example, it's quite clear that something else, a voracious doubt, is driving him to question even the simplest interactions with people. Nothing is authentic for Holden, and his problem is not so much a superficial sorting of the true from the false—he can't figure out how we come to know anything at all. That's the noise, the frightening disturbance in the story, and it will stop only when Holden finds the authentic thing, the real (what?), or when he's too exhausted to continue.

What can Holden rely on, what does he trust, what's real for him? Holden's response to life is, like that of a body in shock, to withdraw into the core of identity, in his case the family, in order to keep the self functioning and alive. There's a love and warmth and security to the way Salinger writes about family, a kind of bulwarked intimacy most readers respond to, that sits in contrast to the false, unfriendly, wolfish world huffing and puffing right outside the door. What I feel reading Salinger is an emotional power that comes from the writer's ingrained assumption of the value and integrity of family, in particular the idea of family defined by siblings. Family is worthy of trust. The siblings in Salinger's work are fiercely loyal and extremely close to one another. So there's that clear separation of family from everyone else, but something in between is missing, some understanding—for the writer, and for Holden. Holden can't negotiate the boundaries between himself and others—Antolini's touch freaks him out—and he can only imagine returning to his family as a refuge. But it's my suspicion that that refuge isn't really a haven the way Holden imagines it—nor is it safe for Salinger, who seems to defang his work by taking the parents out of almost every story. You wonder, where are the adults in this world that's populated almost solely by precocious children?

This is guesswork, this is supposition: the real stress in Holden's life comes from having no safe place, with his family offering him the least security of all. This remains unstated on purpose. In the injunctive first paragraph of *The Catcher in the Rye*, Holden says his parents would have "about two hemorrhages apiece" if he "told anything pretty personal about them. They're quite touchy about anything like that, especially my father. They're *nice* and all—I'm not saying that—but they're also touchy as hell." It's that "touch" rather than Antolini's that's really got Holden running. It should be obvious by now that I don't see *The Catcher in the Rye* as a coming-of-age story, especially not in the dismissive or pejorative sense; to me it's no more about the anxious life of an average teenager than *Huckleberry Finn* is. The feelings Salinger's trying to pinpoint don't really have much to do with the fluctuating moods of a representative teen; adolescence isn't the source of Holden's outsized feelings. Possibly because I came to the book as an adult, for me it's never been about the typical, but rather the exceptional; it's not meant to illustrate a phase of life we all pass through and share but instead to explore a disturbing and extreme loss of identity that leaves this one boy absolutely alone. And the depth of that loss comes from the fact that it's not directly his, but his family's. My guess is that in high school students learn that Holden doesn't go home right away because he knows he's going to be in big trouble. He's been kicked out of school again. He's failed and disappointed his parents once more, and his odyssey through New York is fueled by guilt and contrition. In my reading he doesn't go home after leaving Pencey because home is the problem. His real expulsion is from the family, not school, and his sojourn through New York renders that loss in literal terms: we see the resulting anomie, the thoroughness of his horror. Two very different engines drive the respective readings. In one, he's ultimately headed home, in the other he has nowhere to go, and never will.

Here's the assumption behind my guesswork. Suicide is a kind of death that makes you doubt what you know about the deceased or what you can ever know about anybody. It strikes clear to the core of identity, reaching down into the heart of your life. Since my brother died I haven't slept a single night alone with the lights off; I wake up afraid, and I have to know where I am, I need to see right away. And when I go out, I always leave a radio on, just so that when I come home I'll hear voices or, more precisely, I won't hear the silence and get all spooky imagining the surprises waiting for me. By a curious mechanism my brother's death has extended the vivid fears of my childhood into my adult life. I find that

I'm alert in ways that adults don't need to be, and I'm ignorant of things grown-ups care most about. When a suicide happens within a family, that organism takes on the taint just as much as any individual. But that taint doesn't necessarily mean the dissolution of the family; it might have an opposite effect, banding the family together even more tightly than before. (I felt like shameful secrets had been aired publicly, and I was first of all defensive, protective.) In reality, I think both things happen: you're pulled together, and that intense proximity exposes lines of cleavage that had begun cracking years earlier. The suicide is just a piece finally falling out. And from then on the family's story can't be the same. Its identity must include death, a death shared in the blood. The old narrative breaks at precisely the moment you need it to speak for you. This death, this suicide, is shattering to what, at that exact moment, is your deepest need—family, security, identity.

Rereading Buddy's statement about his ability to detect authenticity, I find a harmonic floating just above the fundamental tone, and I think it can be heard distinctly in isolation here:

For the terrible and undiscountable fact has just reached me, between paragraphs, that I *yearn* to talk, to be queried, to be interrogated, about this particular dead man. *It's just got through to me that, apart from my many other—and, I hope to God, less ignoble—motives, I'm stuck with the usual survivor's conceit that he's the only soul alive who knew the deceased intimately.* [Italics mine.]

This is the overtone you hear in Salinger's work, the knowingness, the high proud insistent certainty, and what accounts for the sound—the instrument, so to speak—is the faculty of mind that's meant to sift through supposed facts and separate the truth from what's false; and the tone is this, the belief that he alone holds the key, the final authentic word on the deceased (or any other matter). The emphasis here is on the belief, not the particular key, whatever it may be. (And I want to make clear that for me this is a musical sound as much as a matter of content. It's what makes *Raise High the Roof Beam, Carpenters* nearly unreadable for me—too much snotty, all-knowing prep-school smugness in the prose, a vague assumption of values, a social vulgarity found in the rich and privileged that's just as revolting, and similar to, the arrogant know-nothingism of the various middle classes, upper to lower. Open the story to almost any page and you can hear the sound in the overpunctuated prose. It's as if the pissy aggrieved prose itself were defending Seymour. You can even hear a trace of the problem in the quote above, in the word "undiscountable"—the leftover locution of a kid putting on adult airs, afraid that someone will realize he doesn't know what he's talking about.) And so, if there really is a single truth, and you alone possess it, there is also, by definition, a lot of falseness out there—the bulk of life, in fact. And this construction, this arrangement or priority, pitting the defense of your holy truth against the entire world's falseness, is suicide refused, refused at least temporarily.

And it's silence refused, too.

Here's what I mean. A long-standing and widely accepted formulation is that suicide is redirected homicide. Edwin Shneidman, the father of the modern study of suicide, coined the phrase: "Suicide is murder in the 180th degree." There are variations on this, of course. Suicide's not always—probably never—an act of pure hostility. There's a fairly old article by Ives Hendrick of the Harvard Medical School that argues the case for suicide as a form of identification with the lost love object, a fantasy of reunion rather than murder, and while this thinking doesn't occupy a place in the fat mainstream of suicidology, it is accepted, a tributary that helps explain some cases. I'm throwing these ideas out scattershot, hoping to indicate a central

theme within the wide range of psychodynamic meanings attributed to suicide: that it's always accompanied
by some shift away from life's normal priority, where
it's perfectly natural and expected that you'd defend
yourself from danger, to a condition where you give
up, defenseless, or even join in on the attack. In Freud's
still fascinating "Mourning and Melancholia," he begins by openly admitting to being flummoxed by suicide and the self's attack on itself. He says the ego is
usually fierce and robust in the protection of itself, ral-
lying the troops when under siege, so how or why does
ego-functioning break down and become defenseless
in the suicide? In short, the self can hate the self to
the point of suicide only when a lost internalized object—an object, moreover, of love—turns against the
self. In other words, it's your inner daddy—protected
by your love of him—messing with your defenseless
inner child—or whatever, some variation of that. Later
(1933) Karl Menninger develops his triadic theory of
suicide—the wish to die, the wish to kill, the wish to
be killed—to which, years afterward, he speculated
on the need to add a fourth condition, the wish to be
loved—and he talks about a mechanism by which the
suicide's "hostile component, since it would otherwise
have to be directed against the whole world, is turned
inward upon the self." I'm really oversimplifying here,

reducing complex theories into these candied bits, and I'm skipping the work of so many, of Maltsberger, Hendin, Leenaars, Jamison, etc., but I'm trying to get at something, this general tendency in suicide, that will bring us back to Salinger.

In suicide, then, a couple of the main poles of life flip, and the desire to talk or communicate turns into a longing for a colossal silence (most suicides don't write a note), and the fierce defense of the self becomes an equally fierce and final defeat. It's like the mind, exhausted by the enormous work of defending itself, turns around out of some need for efficiency or economy, and begins hating itself, doubting or attacking its reality. Being suicidal *is* really tiring. A lot of suicides are so lacking in affect and so lethargic that they aren't able to kill themselves until their mood improves—spring, for that reason, has the highest rate of what people in the business call "completed" suicides. The ego first tries to protect itself and then can't, in part because to do so would be to attack a forbidden love object. (Buddy Glass says he can't finish writing a description of Seymour, "even a bad description, even one where my ego, my perpetual lust to share top billing with him, is all over the place"—making a sideways admission of jealousy and also expressing resentment for the sainted brother he can no longer defeat and no

longer even describe without desecration.) What's salient in *The Catcher in the Rye* is that Holden achieves
a fragile truce between hating himself and hating the
world. Holden Caulfield is probably identified in the
minds of most readers as a boy whose anger at and suspicion of the world is fragilely offset by his inviolate
love for Allie and Phoebe. As long as he keeps that love
immaculate, as long as he defends and protects it and
maintains its purity, he's alive, and that's what I mean
by suicide refused. Holden without his holy love is a
goner, and the unalloyed quality of that love is really the
register of his isolation. He's cornered, and you can see
the gargantuan project he's set for himself, that vast defense. In the novel he ends up in an institution, which
isn't really a lasting solution to his problem but instead
a sort of DMZ between himself and the world.

Similarly, Buddy Glass, a writer (in two other institutions, the military and the academy—and all these
institutions, these supporting structures, stand in for a
neutral family), asserts his identity by claiming close inner knowledge of his dead brother, Seymour. His relation to Seymour is sacerdotal and similar to the Holden
Antolini says he can imagine dying nobly for an unwor-
thy cause. But even in the passage quoted and italicized
above, in the middle of his assertion, Buddy's already
begun to undermine it, calling it a "conceit," an instance

of cleverness that, but for the writer's vigilance, would have hardened into a fixed posture, would have become false, phony. And I would argue that only a little farther down this line of thinking we come to the idea that all writing, fixed on the page, claiming truth, is false. It's imaginable that a writer, in the wake of a suicide, might find all coherent narratives suspect, all postures false, and, looking at life up close under a new magnifying hypervigilance, might finally come to question and mistrust the integrity of his own inventions as well. The word "conceit" cancels Buddy's claim to know Seymour, dismissing it and sending it on its way toward silence. And silence—a kind of reunion with Seymour, or a way to equal or defeat him, head to head, silence for silence—is one possible response to this powerful but confused idea of falsity. If *The Catcher in the Rye* is noisy in its search for authenticity, then the rest of Salinger's work looks for the real by stilling the very engine that drives Holden's vast doubt—words. And this silence is related to and yet something beyond the interest in Zen quietude that crops up in Salinger's later work.

Holden's isolation in an institution as he tells his story points to a formal problem Salinger himself seems to have resolved through withdrawal and writerly silence. At least it's tempting to see it that way. I've poked around in all the work for prodromal clues somehow indicating Salinger's plunge into silence was symptomatic of something. What is the silence about? In some people (usually willful or grandiose or highly defended types) there's only a very small difference between talking incessantly and saying nothing. I vaguely remember a quote from Roland Barthes, who claimed his rhetorical needs alternated between a little haiku that expressed everything and a great flood of banalities that said nothing. And in *Seymour: An Introduction*, Buddy Glass says of his brother, "Vocally, he was either as brief as a gatekeeper at a Trappist monastery—sometimes for days, weeks at a stretch—or he was a non-stop talker." Interestingly, *The Catcher in the Rye*, Salinger's most voluble book, begins and ends with specific comments concerning what will *not* be written.

Holden starts his story with a refusal: "If you really want to hear about it, the first thing you'll probably want to know is where I was born, and what my lousy childhood was like, and how my parents were occupied and all before they had me, and all that David Copperfield kind of crap, but I don't feel like going into it, if you want to know the truth." And he ends the novel with this hardened commandment: "Don't ever tell anybody anything. If you do, you start missing everybody."

The quotes above bracket the book, suggesting prohibitions of both point of view and content. Holden will not look at the life of his parents or take the tack of examining his past or childhood—this is no remembrance—and by the end of the novel his instinct, in a sense, proves him right, proves that the process of writing only creates further problems. He's not newly wise like Nick Carraway. He has no new perspective or understanding. The only thing Holden seems to learn from telling even this restricted story is that, confirming his first hunch, it would have been better to say nothing.

Silence is already there, waiting in the wings of Salinger's most clamorous and fluent book.

Is silence for a writer tantamount to suicide? In some ways it is, I believe, but the question for me is why— why does the writer choose silence? The deliberate decision to quit clawing at the keyboard is too mechanical to be an answer. Stopping isn't the real matter, but rather the result of some other prior disturbance that can't be named. Silence in this sense isn't the equivalent of suicide or death, but of secrecy. That's what it's about— what is not said. Taking Salinger's oeuvre as a unified field I find a couple of elements that don't square with either my experience or my avocational reading in the literature of suicide—elements where a silence rules. He never really looks at the role of parents in family

life, and never examines, in particular, their position
re: Seymour's suicide. It's a substantial omission, and
perhaps not an omission at all but instead a protective
silence. I don't know, and on this point I don't care to
speculate beyond the observation that, in general, people
from good, functioning families rarely kill themselves.
And in crappy, broken-down families a child's attention
is often focused on nothing but the parents. Suffice it to
say there's something big missing in Salinger's account.
And the other thing not present in Salinger's work is outright anger toward Seymour or a sense of doubt about
him. As Buddy describes him Seymour has no flaws, and
to me the absence of flaws and of anger and doubt is a
texture that's conspicuously missing. Why? I can't say,
although I feel the effects. In *Seymour: An Introduction,*
Buddy never lets the reader forget that he, Buddy, is sitting alone at his desk, writing. It's all just writing, he
wants us to know, the lumber of it, the cut and stacked
phrases, the punctuation nailed to the paper, the parentheses put up to frame different doubts, etc.—as if to
say this project, this monument under construction, will
always fall short of honoring the actual character. Where
Holden insists on Phoebe's innocence and pretty easily
posits an idea of her essence, Buddy sees past his brother
into the conceits and constructions that create him on
the page. And because of this, perhaps, Seymour never

251

feels real, never seems to emerge from the workbench of the writer, to live and walk among men.

The writer won't or can't let him die:

> What I *am*, I think, is a thesaurus of undetached prefatory remarks about him. I believe I essentially remain what I've almost always been—a narrator, but one with extremely pressing personal needs. I want to introduce, I want to describe, I want to distribute mementos, amulets, I want to break out my wallet and pass around snapshots, I want to follow my nose.

Here again you get a kind of intense identification with Seymour, one that blocks Buddy's way—he's "undetached," he has "pressing personal needs," and because of this he can only make "prefatory" remarks. The isolated "I *am*" is telling; with the comma where it is, the weight of the sentence remains stuck to the subject, rather than shifting forward via the verb to its object. The "I *am*" seems open-ended, perpetual. (Is time taken out of the sentence because the writer won't let history happen, won't let his character die? It's curious that in a life that's ended, that's so emphatically finished, the writer can't begin, can't offer anything more than an introduction. Would finishing Seymour mean outliving him? Or the converse: Does failing to finish Seymour leave him alive?) The identity thing here is ruthless, close, smothering, endless. Consider that quote and the problem when set beside this:

> I privately say to you, old friend (unto you, really, I'm afraid), please accept from me this unpretentious bouquet of very early-blooming parentheses: (((()))). I suppose, most unflorally, I truly mean them to be taken, first off, as bowlegged— buckle-legged—omens of my state of mind and body at this writing.

There's that cowardly, obfuscating "un-" construction— "unpretentious," "unflorally"—cropping up again (which nearly always works as a mask, sneaky and meaning the very opposite of what it states, meaning, in this case, *pretentious, floral*), but the point now is to draw attention to the parentheses. (Although in working through various drafts of this essay I realized my second paragraph was full of precisely this construction, the *un* prefix with its absences and canceled actions. It appears five times, and occupies the privileged, key position as the last word in the paragraph: *unbitten.* It crossed my mind to correct the problem by burying it in some low geological stratum of the piece, but I haven't. There's that desire in writing, as in life, to rewind everything after a suicide, to return to some pristine moment, and so in this too Salinger is *mon frère, mon semblable*.) The parentheses sit like Kevlar jackets all through the writing, protecting Buddy's identity from attack, keeping the sentences safe. *Seymour: An Introduction* is like a story in hiding, its prose on the lam, its characters putting on disguises, its ideas concealed. The whole thing is preambular, it's all excursus, and it's a bad sign that for me the best or most accurate language for describing the story comes from classical rhetoric and oratory. The sentences spin eloquently over an absence—it's as if progress has stopped, and the last few words are draining out. Earlier I said that Holden is making a loud shouted appeal directly to the audience, over the heads of those who don't understand. The whole story is directed at you, the reader. In *Seymour*, Buddy Glass speaks directly to the reader too, but now he resorts to the aside, the isolated whispered phrase, safely enclosed in parentheses, addressing the audience in a low voice supposedly inaudible to others nearby.

Who is nearby?

I know: his brother.

Salinger isn't primarily a funny writer, and humor, except sporadically in *The Catcher in the Rye*, is largely absent from his work. His primary thing is empathy, the yearning for it, the hope and the need, both as a giver and receiver. Buddy's desire for empathic union with his brother is single-minded and loyal and makes for an interesting case, but Seymour never finally comes to life. The book is one long stutter and a fascinating failure. Buddy can't write Seymour because, when he tries, Seymour fragments and falls apart—you get the parts, you get the eyes, the nose, the voice, etc. He wants his brother so bad, it's a sad thing to watch, to see Seymour breaking to pieces in Buddy's hands. The Salinger I've been discussing seems at times to feel he's got a corner on the Truth, this unwieldy lump he keeps hidden like the kid with the secret goldfish in D. B.'s story, who won't show it to anybody because he bought it with his own money. Perhaps this Truth is centrally important because the suicide takes his secret with him, and it's easy to get caught up in a monomaniacal search for the Answer, pinning your painfully vast hope to a single Idea. Up to a point, you believe the person who killed himself took the ultimate truth, and life afterward often feels like a sorrowful search for that last, unknown key to the life, which will explain everything. The paradox is that this hope or need for certainty seems to make the world less stable. The belief in a single Truth leads to doubt about everything. The need for empathic union makes the actual separation just terribly, terribly huge.

When we shift the relationship away from Buddy-Seymour to Salinger-Holden, then, as an act of writing, Salinger's empathy for Holden Caulfield makes *The Catcher in the Rye* something special, an intense and fierce and intimate look at a character who arouses in readers—me, let's say—a level of sympathetic identification nearly equal to the one felt for Fitzgerald's Gatsby.

After my brother's death I felt I had too much feeling to be myself. I felt attacked by my emotions, under siege, and the sensation, day after day, was like life had stuck to me. Like it was pinned to my back. This whatever, this stab of feeling, probably influenced the fate of the doomed robin. I could have stood by until the crow killed it, or sat still until somebody a little more altruistic came down the street and stepped in to save it, rushing the bird off to a Humane Society shelter; or someone else could have come down the street, this time in a car, and run it over. Lots of things could have happened. But instead I scooped the bird up in my Filson cap, folding the hat like a taco shell so it couldn't escape, and carried it to a vacant lot with a weedy path that led down to the lake. For some reason I thought the crow might follow us, but crows are comical birds and that one's interest had already moved on to something new. I walked into the murky water of Lake Union, my mind blank, and, bending down, dunked the hat under. The bird was still trying to fly, brushing its one good wing against the fabric, and when that stopped I pulled my hat away. The robin floated to the surface, lifelessly riding the tiny waves, and I smacked the hat against my leg, knocking beads of water off the waxed cotton. I picked a few gray feathers from the inner brim and put the hat on, looking west across the water to the Aurora Bridge. And while now the bridge reminds me of my brother Mike, comically pratfalling through an indifferent universe, back then it made me think of Danny, tragically dead at twenty-one after shooting himself in my bedroom.

With Danny, years have passed and I still feel a deathly guilt. I never did anything but love my brother and that wasn't enough. And now every breath I take is a betrayal, a refusal of his choice. It's not sentimental indulgence, it's not so much that I ask myself what happened to the hand I held in crosswalks, but rather that I cross all those streets again. I stay with him now, I'm *always* nearby. I am always ten and he is always three, and I sit in the kitchen spooning canned peas into his mouth, swallowing most of them myself, and he gets a bowl of spumoni for being a good boy and eating his vegetables. I'm with him and I never feel like I belong entirely to present-day life. I've never really held a serious job or applied myself to anything worthwhile, I'm an unreliable, shitty friend, and I've never loved anyone deeply or satisfactorily. Killing the robin was an early experiment in grieving and acceptance that didn't work too well. I knew the bird had no life ahead of it and I wanted to anticipate that doom rather than stand off at a safe distance. I didn't want to be uncertain. But where before I had too much feeling, after drowning the bird I felt nothing, I was indifferent, I was remorseless. I thought I could rejoin the universe by being cruel and unfeeling, but obviously I was having trouble with focal distance and zeroing in on the exact right place where most of life was happening.

Here is a quote from Dietrich Bonhoeffer that I treasure for capturing one side of how I feel. It gets me closer to acceptance and understanding than anything else. It's from his *Letters and Papers from Prison*, and was written, I think, at a time when he knew he would die in the concentration camp, so he speaks from inside the heart of his death.

Nothing can make up for the absence of someone whom we love, and it would be wrong to try to find a substitute; we must simply hold out and see it through. That sounds very hard at first, but at the same time it is a great consolation, for the gap, as long as it remains unfilled, preserves the bonds between us. It is nonsense to say that God fills the gap; He doesn't fill it, but on the contrary, He keeps it empty and so helps us to keep alive our former communion with each other, even at the cost of pain.

From the get-go, my brother Mike's suicide attempt struck me as a piece of comedy. Maybe that's because it came to me like the comedian's idea of the topper, the rule that says you follow up a good joke with a second, even better joke. Keep them laughing! Maybe it's because I always picture Mike tumbling haplessly through space, and falls are a staple of comedy and clowning, as is anything that turns the body into an object. Maybe it's because when he jumped over the rail he was being chased by the devil and then he was aware, halfway down, that the devil was gone and he was all alone, falling like a rock. Or maybe, as in *King Lear*, it's just too much, and the wise man sees life like the fool and laughs; either that or he cracks. Mike was really wrecked-up, his body broken, and when I saw him at the VA hospital he had nuts and bolts and this kind of light-gauge medical rebar rising like scaffolding from his smashed pelvis. His right shoulder was immobilized, so that, in combination with the broken pelvis, and his ruined bladder, which was being drained by a catheter, he seemed like just another malfunctioning contraption or a Rube Goldberg contrivance. At home we always had old jalopy equipment like black-and-white televisions with no horizontal hold, and our cars were ancient and unreliable and broken-down—in one of our cars the transmission would overheat and the carpet in the backseat would catch fire and smolder on any drive longer than ten miles, so we did the obvious thing, we kept a jug of water in the car. In the hospital Mike looked to me like just another one of our crappy busted things, where the attempt at repair was funny in a way that the initial problem was not. Whereas I remember helping Danny eat his peas, I remember laughing at Mike as he tried to get a hamburger to his mouth. I sat in a chair and watched. He couldn't do it—you can't sit up straight with a broken pelvis—and his mouth and the hamburger just hung there, apart from each other, it seemed, for all time.

And so over here, Henri Bergson's essay on the comic suggests another side, a possible path for me in my ongoing attempt to understand life by reading books:

I would point out . . . the *absence of feeling* which usually accompanies laughter. . . . Indifference is its natural environment, for laughter has no greater foe than emotion. . . . In a society composed of pure intelligences there would probably be no more tears, though perhaps there would still be laughter; whereas highly emotional souls, in tune and unison with life, in whom every event would be sentimentally prolonged and re-echoed, would neither know nor understand laughter.

Put in a slightly different way, it was Charlie Chaplin, I think, who said that life up close is a tragedy, but from a distance it's a comedy. Somebody slipping on a banana peel is still funny, unless it's you. And the genius of Salinger is that, speaking through Holden Caulfield, highly emotional, in tune and unison with life, with events re-echoing still, he told us exactly what it feels like to feel too much. ❖

Misreading

Brooklyn.

I had to borrow money to make the move. This was long ago, in a vanished world, when my father was still alive. I was standing outside his den, waiting, because when I'd knocked on his door he'd lifted a silencing finger to signal that he was in the middle of something important, some business. So characteristic, that gesture, the air of preoccupation. It always hurt, even though I understood that it was theater, like a frozen pose in Kabuki. Now he's gone, gone for good, and only my memory of the gesture remains, a knot of puzzled meaning that chokes off other sympathies.

When I was fourteen I'd asked him about premarital sex because I knew it was out there, in the offing, and

I was looking for guidance. I was hoping for a path out of Catholicism, a loophole in the homiletics I knew by heart. I put my question in a note because that's what we did when the matter was difficult—we wrote it down. We thought it through and considered the alternatives and then we made a careful plea. Eventually he'd write back, sometimes by hand, often typed. The waiting was murder. We swapped these notes in cubbyholes, a grid of wooden boxes like you'd see in the lobby of an old hotel. The cubbies were by the kitchen, and you'd check them like it was Delphi, to see if the Oracle had gotten around to your business. Communicating this way might seem quaint or curious, the sort of departmentalism that develops in response to managing seven kids, but here's what happened: it kept us quiet. Our deepest concerns were treated as secrets, and our needs, sealed in envelopes, felt illicit. In time my father wrote back, telling me that he didn't believe in premarital sex, nor did he believe in extramarital sex. His response had the rote sound of the Baltimore Catechism. I had been hoping for something more lifelike. A week later I banged my thirteen-year-old girlfriend on a dusty bed in her basement without birth control.

My father pulled out his ledger and wrote a check to cover a one-way ticket. He handed me the check but didn't ask any questions, didn't seem to register that

I was at a juncture in my life and that I might need something more than a loan and our usual silence. A few weeks later I left Seattle for Brooklyn, casting my lot with a woman I knew to be a liar and a cheat.

I think it goes, "You can never get enough of what you don't want." I've taped the spine together but the pages fall out anyway; flipping through them in search of the exact quote is like shuffling a deck of cards. It's a cheap edition, a pocketbook that would have originally been sold in a drugstore, the cover a little too loud, clamorous in a lime-green jacket meant to compete with pomades and hairpins. In 1971 it cost $1.50. Striking a cautionary note, the copy on the cover says that it's "the highly provocative best-selling analysis of the fanatic, a man compelled to join a cause, any cause . . ."

The book belongs to the precocious childhood of my brother, who once read all of Plato's *Republic* to my mother, a few pages every night before bed. He was twelve then. He was that kid. Though I was older, I admired him, saw something rare and auspicious in his intelligence. I'd brag to friends, reading those signs, seeing prophecy in his hungry mind, but as the years wore on, as my brother ran away, as he stole and pawned our tiny treasures, as he turned seventeen and joined the marines, as he went UA and hit the bush and lived on a meridian strip on I-5, as he was discharged (honorably) and then locked away in the VA mental ward on Beacon Hill, as his life became ever more shadowy until the shadows alone were real, only then did I change my tune and come to understand that reading the *Republic* at age twelve was not a sign but a symptom, not an augury at all but an alarm, one that could hardly have been any clearer.

Somewhere along the way I inherited my brother's copy of *The True Believer*. It was Eric Hoffer's first book, and I saw in it—and in Hoffer himself—what my brother must have seen—a familiar face, a face you could trust. Hoffer had the roughed-up look of someone we'd seen around. A character out of our childhood, wandered up from the waterfront, grandfathered in. A stevedore, his right thumb destroyed, the collar of his wool coat turned up against the cold. I read that book in a single sitting, I read it and I romanced it. Hoffer spoke to me, he looked me in the eye and addressed me directly, each sentence delivered like a confidence, a matter of deep mutual trust. But I also happened to be that true believer, that fanatic, the man compelled to join a cause, any cause . . .

The actual quotation reads: "They demonstrate the fact that we can never have enough of that which we really do not want, and that we run fastest and farthest when we run from ourselves."

Our whole time together she was less a girlfriend than a hypothesis, a vague guess at the truth, in constant need of testing and verification, further research. Before Brooklyn, we'd arranged to live abroad, in Paris, but as soon as I arrived she said she wanted to go to Geneva. When I agreed to go, she said she needed time alone, and the very next morning she packed a bag and left for Barcelona with someone else. After we parted ways, I was sure I'd never see her again. But then she called me, she called and we talked, and suddenly I was waiting outside the door of my father's den, standing there, hoping he might help me out.

She took a job as the assistant to the producer of a movie, and by the time I got to Brooklyn she was fucking the director. Two weeks later she hired a helicopter for her brother's birthday, and a party of movie people flew off the roof of some building in Manhattan to see the city from above. I hadn't been invited, though I had been lied to, meaning I knew. Her lies embarrassed me because I could see them. I remember looking up at the sky a lot that Sunday afternoon. The whole time I lived in the city, drifting from borough to borough, I never once saw a helicopter without wondering if that was her, if she was in it.

I knew she was lying to me, but that doesn't mean I knew what was true. In this way, our relationship had the character of a rumor, something I'd heard about, something I knew only secondhand. Still, we managed to resemble a couple for a while. I'm not sure who we were imitating. Even in the passionate throes of youth, we kept up appearances, but the fit was poor and awkward and I kind of suspect people saw through the charade. I certainly felt as if people could see right through me, like I had no substance, like every tiny wheel, every whirring mechanism, every ratchet and pawl were visible.

That I can't say with any degree of certainty whether her apartment was in Cobble Hill or Boerum Hill or Carroll Gardens indicates something about the radical disorientation I felt in those days. Even now, the names of those neighborhoods sound far-off and dreamy. I remember them coming up in conversation with an almost incantatory insistence, but the borders they were meant to mark—the classes they created, the hopes they defined, the precise distinctions they were meant to articulate—completely escaped me. I know all of it mattered; it just didn't matter to me.

Every lie breaks the world in two, it divides the narrative, and eventually I fell through a crack into the subplot, becoming a minor character in my own life. The surrendering felt much like the blackening of consciousness just before you faint, the letting go, the acceptance, and whatever was good in me turned passive and strange. I knew happy love had no history, and it seemed that any history, no matter how sordid, was better than none. I stayed in the story, and we went on resembling, while I roamed in a world of lesser importance. And in that exile, far from the main action, Brooklyn welcomed me.

I felt at home on subway platforms, down in the heat and stink, waiting for trains, because people avoided eye contact and no single line of vision ever tangled. Those tiny evasions turned us into strangers, and the shifty desperate feel had a dramatic pressure, like a standoff, but always, just when the tension rose to a certain pitch, a train would come and carry us off by the carload. Up on the streets it was like a foreign country. I never understood where anyone was going. Every window on every bus seemed to frame a lonely face. I walked everywhere but I was always lost. People would clot up and form groups that I couldn't fully comprehend but figured were probably families. The only face that passed for familiar was an ancient Italian woman I saw making her rounds, an old widow in black who shopped for groceries, pushing an antique pram up the aisles, her soda crackers and kippered fish and milk nestled in blankets.

One morning I found a church, St. Charles Borromeo, and I went in because he's my patron saint. I lowered a kneeler in one of the pews, and just being there with the slightly damp smell of cold stones and the familiar emptiness made me want to confess. Mass was ending but the responsorial chant, the intonation of every line, was recognizable to me from rhythms I had learned as a child. At early weekday masses it's always Eleanor Rigby and her devout sisters, the secret sufferers, the wounded, the inconsolable, women who show up in their hastily tied bonnets and tattered housecoats, each alone, scattered through the nave, and yet that morning their thin muffled voices held so near to the note and so exactly to those rising and falling rhythms I knew by heart that joining in with them was like letting someone else do my breathing for a while. I had not felt so close to anyone in ages.

Ahead of me the devout prepared their conscience to make a good confession. Bowed heads, closed eyes, and those tough hands, squared off, blunted by the life they'd handled, now folded and resting together. I was calm, breathing deeply, but when I closed my eyes to make a tally of my own venial sins, I could track only random images. There was a day in Brooklyn Heights, along the promenade, when I watched a baby, crawling in diapers, pick a cigarette butt off the ground and eat it. I wasn't sure what to do, I lived at such a distance from others and from myself. I walked away. Or there was the day I found myself standing on a bridge over a slough of crud, watching two kids toss rocks at the carcass of a dog as the tide slowly dragged it away. I didn't know where I was, but later I would describe it to people and everyone guessed I was down in a place they called the Gowanus Gulch. I know this is my essay, but does such a place even exist? In the church I watched the women come and go through the confessional and then walk to the altar and kneel and cross themselves and do their penance but when it was my time, I left, not because I was without sin but because I had lost the habit of truth. All I had was this story of walking around, of going no-where, and I would not know where to begin. Someone else would have to tell me. ❖

Casting Stones

The King County Regional Justice Center is a kind of justice multiplex and includes under one roof a jail, courts, probation stuff, covered parking, all the amenities. Outside the parking garage on a patch of sloping lawn there's a sculpture garden with a Native American motif—big trinkets of rebar bent to look like teepees, arrows, some kind of mandala/dream catcher thing, a piscine shape, etc. Looking at it you feel less in the elevated presence of art than hammered over the head by a governmental or bureaucratic intention, and the effect is of Sovietized realism, of culture that's policed, official, approved, frozen, clichéd, one-note, panderly, in other words, everything that art is not.

Winding past this display of agitprop is a path lined with lampposts whose fixtures are a kitsch rendition of the scales of justice. That path leads to a glass door with an ingenious pneumatic device that replicates good manners by holding the door open for you and, after a polite interval perfectly timed to let you in, shutting it quietly behind you, and once inside, you find a seamless continuation of the same orthodox themes, the same didacticism, the same blunt clarity of signs as in the bush-league art outside. Just about everywhere you turn there's a placard that tells you what to do or not do. The hallways are full of instruction. Press to Open. No Smoking. No Weapons Allowed. No guns, no knives, no chemical sprays, etc. For Public Safety the use of skateboards roller skates roller blades Strictly Prohibited. Please use revolving doors. Eviction info in rm 1B/1100. Men. Women. (Generic bathroom symbols, with gender distinguished by skirt (girls), pants (boys).) You feel squeezed by subtext, monitored like a child in class, but you also wonder a little what evil alien race of cartoon figures comes here in need of so much explicit guidance. Probably a lot of the people entering the RJC have demonstrated an impaired ability to read the signs out in society and maybe that explains the need for Mosaic clarity. The signs steer the daily stream of prevaricators in the right direction for once.

In a windowed rotunda there's a guy with a red feather duster dusting away at 7:00 AM. He doesn't seem to come by dusting naturally; there's a dispirited vo-tech or occupational therapy aspect to the way he does the job, a trained make-work quality, a lack of flair, especially when he starts dusting the walls. The walls! I keep watching and wondering what dust has fallen on this immaculate place in the night. It looks like he's trying to catch the dust in flight, before it lands. Preventive dusting. I watch him wave the duster and I listen to the shoptalk of journalists. It sounds really important having this proximal relation to reality, living every day of your life as the next-door neighbor to the truth. After a while the courtroom opens and the big fish in the media pool are ushered in and seated so they'll get the clearest view (camera angle) of Mary Kay Letourneau when the time comes. Myself, I'm seated right behind the family of the young man I'll call X^1 and who for legal and dramatic purposes the press has labeled a "boy" or a "child" or a "victim." When Letourneau enters stage left and sits beside her lawyer, I have an obstructed view of the back of her head. At my age I've seen the backs of untold thousands of heads—more backs

---

1 No longer a secret, X = Vili Fualaau

than fronts, probably—and note nothing particularly interesting to say about hers.

Mary Kay Letourneau dared to be unclear in public. "I wish," she said, "there was a story that made sense and could be told right now, but there isn't." When she arrived in court for the sentencing she had a frail wispy etiolated look from having spent months in jail but otherwise her in-person face showed the same smudged and incoherent prettiness captured in countless pictures. I'd seen plenty of those photos in the papers and magazines and with each instance I wondered why her features weren't in focus. But it turns out they were; it's just that her face, even in real life, appears clouded and dreamy and somewhat removed from the immediate scene. Her lawyer, David Gehrke, characterized her as a woman with "a screw loose" who "doesn't know how to separate reality and fantasy." Her husband, Steve Letourneau, for some ulterior reason wanted everybody to know she was not Mary Poppins. In my experience the strategy a lot of frightened women turn to is that of making themselves intangible. Rather than go hard and confrontational the way a man in crisis might, they become ethereal and really remote. Based on no one's authority but my own, I would say Letourneau showed the mien of a battered woman, of someone in retreat from her own face, whose safe haven is inward, reclusive, solitary, distant, and that what you saw in the pictures, in the photographed face the press captioned variously as belonging in an abstract allegoric uppercase way to a Wife, a Teacher, a Mother, was little more than a mask she'd vacated a long time ago.

She wasn't clear. She insisted until she was silenced by lawyer Gehrke and pressured by the public call for a kowtowing show of remorse and civic obedience that her relationship with X was love. She said that "given the nature of this situation—and that includes the charges against me, the media, everything—there isn't anything *within legal bounds* that I can say to help make sense of what is happening." (My italics.) Against the chorus of experts who in one rote voice claimed her relationship with X was "distortion" and "manipulation" and "rationalization," Letourneau said, "I would not expect people to understand, but it did exist and it was real." She was never loose or gallionic about the gravity of her situation and her public statements always struck me as honest and unfiltered, a too frank, badly lawyered expression of confusion that rang true, not because she was successful in justifying or rationalizing her actions, but precisely because she was hesitant, uncertain, floundering—precisely because she failed, and failed publicly! She never told us what we wanted to hear. She wasn't glib, she wasn't corny, she never once deliberately lied or even delivered a pat, practiced answer. Given the boundaries she'd crossed and the taboos she'd broken and the generally undone state of her life, it's incredible to me she was even able to speak at all. The story drew prurient attention locally and from around the country, and soon after that the experts moved in with their extra-strength vocabularies, the proficient idioms of the law, of social work, of psychology, but Letourneau alone seemed to have trouble finding words. You could hear in her voice and in the absence of cant that her true feelings, whatever they were, like Cordelia's love, were more ponderous than her tongue.

Pretty much the opposite of Letourneau's hesitance was the insta-commentary offered up by local broadcasters. After the sentencing one Bonnie Hart from KIRO or KOMO—I forget which and don't believe it really matters—quickly convened a kind of radio Sanhedrin. As far as I know Hart's only real qualification for commenting on Letourneau is that she holds a job that requires her to say something re: something most every day of the week. Day after day I suppose she's paid to be fluent in politics, cookbooks, fresh vegetables, fads, open or closed batting stances, menopause, studded tires, whatever. In other words, her authority is mostly occupational, though it seems she's possessed of omni-science. Her opinions weren't suasive enough to win me over, not by any of the common measures I developed as a Catholic kid avidly listening for lame moments in hundreds of homilies. No elegance or force of thought, no wit, no keen insight, no revelatory moments that broadened perspectives, that enlivened feelings, no reso-nance, no self-scrutiny, no risk, no compassion or sym-pathy or anything close to eloquence. By the strident and aggressive tenor of the talk you couldn't tell if this Bonnie Hart entertained any doubt, then or ever, she was so careful not to cross herself, so careful to arrange her moral outrage along the lines of least resistance. In a sense the whole program was about Hart rendering the round world flat and endorsing lopsidedness, halfness. This seemed a crude and retrogressive project, since what really distinguishes us from apes is not the oppos-able thumb but the ability to hold in mind opposing ideas, a distinction we should probably try to preserve.

But these days you get the impression people think it's kind of recreant to waver, as if by feeling and ex-pressing, or worst of all admitting, doubt and uncer-tainty, you're being disloyal to a guiding idea. In the case of Mary Kay Letourneau it seemed to me that over the previous nine months what you had was the spectacle of this woman who'd been publicly knocked down, disgraced, humiliated, scorned, abandoned, who'd been imprisoned and made destitute, who'd lost everything, her family, her job, her house, her reputation, her freedom, her privacy, and even if I accepted the hardest line of the moral hard-liners, even allowing for the possibility that this "adulterous" and "abusive" woman deserved what she got, that her crimes were staggering and odious and the probationary sentence just handed down by Judge Linda Lau was too lenient, that didn't stop me from feeling uncomfortable and real lonely as I listened to this brave and pharisaic Bonnie Hart, who from the safe defilade of her radio booth was basically bending over to pick up the first stone.

In a "situation" like this it's worth considering why only the authorities, the experts, the credentialed explainers remain articulate. Anyone alive today has at his or her disposal ages of mental experience to draw upon, and yet we seem to trust and accept only the most recent orthodoxies, the latest theories, the newest and freshest ideas in the marketplace. I applaud this reliance on the red-hot and the new when it comes to landing airplanes or doing appendectomies. Elsewhere, however, it seems we're just skimming the surface to locate the most recently revised version of ourselves—a tentative, experimental understanding. A long backward glance establishes pretty clearly what's endured over time and also exposes a lot of discredited stuff that was once taken quite seriously. I'm not just talking about the obvious crackpots and charlatans, nor do I mean the briefly credible phrenologists and lobotomists and such, but rather the discarded, the outmoded, the no-longer tenable, like, say, the Ptolemaic astronomers and the reign of geocentrists that lasted a long two millennia. Even Marx and Freud, our last two great systematizers, show signs of wear and exhaustion after just a single century of application. Experts in every field hold holy models and systems, languages, under-standings, that are themselves subject to challenge, re-vamping, innovation, further sectarian squabbles, and so the whole reeling thing bravely wobbles on, even under the administration of people whose intentions are of the highest order. They're dedicated. They keep up. Offices around this city are right now jammed with journals, trade publications, notes for papers and lec-tures, a whirlwind schedule of symposia stretching out over the upcoming calendar year, whatever, but it's not really possible (nor really desirable) to declare finality of understanding within a single discipline.

And so we improve one prejudice to rest awhile in another, we embrace errors, we correct, reverse ear-lier decisions, advance again, struggle pitifully, and meantime as we revise and roll on, Letourneau is caught in the amber of our understanding. This sense of understanding as fossil sample occurred throughout the story, and after many readings of just about everything written on the Letourneau case I entered a near-mad state of chicken/egg confusion where habitual priority starts flipping around, and I couldn't tell anymore if people were trying to understand and describe Letourneau or invent a theoretical prototype. I started being unable to understand the words people were using, I couldn't make sense of *trust* and *manipulation* and *adultery* and *power base* and *exploitation* and *teacher*, and other than seeing this as ample evidence of why I'm not a judge or a lawyer or a doctor or a cop or for that matter anybody with any meaningful responsibility or position in this world, and getting a real sorrowful glimpse of why that's probably a very good thing, I also began to believe that of course Letourneau had to be sentenced, that sentencing her was a way of stabilizing the language. She upset accepted meaning (and by the way I have no problem with Judge Lau's decision. That's not my concern here). What I wonder about is language, about what gets lost when laypeople concede the control of words to clinicians, scientists, lawyers, etc., which is, scilicet, the rich, supple instrumentation of language that makes it an encounter with reality, that lets it reach into everything, into every little part of life, and how in this case a circle had formed and experts with fixed language were returning Letourneau to a fixed state, and doing so by excluding, again and again, notions that were not naturally a part of their descriptive vocabulary, like love.

Even though in the following quote I'm cutting a little bit against the grain of her intention, I think Lucy Berliner of Harborview Medical Center framed the problem succinctly when she said, "Even if [Letourneau] does genuinely have feelings for him, there is no context for a relationship like this to be normalized."

No context, where? In the language of sociology, law, psychology, victimology, penology, pedagogy? And what's "a relationship like *this*"? What's the omitted word? And why select the evasive, hesitant, nonspecific word "feelings"? And why the qualifier "even if"? And what's the difference between saying "even if she does *genuinely* have feelings for him" and saying "even if she has *genuine* feelings for him"? (Opting for the weak adverb instead of the adjectival form basically cripples Letourneau's action and in subtle syntactic ways indicates her feelings were never genuine or real in the object-noun world but only in her head, a shift in the direction of subjectivity that feeds right into the psych-soc agenda, the fixing up or at least identifying of errant bad-acting people with defective heads. It's all very neat and circular, and the system of Berliner's sentence is well-tuned.)

But right now this is Einstein's world and both trains are moving, so I want to go back briefly and look at the idea of the discarded. This is pretty common in the sciences, the abandoning of paradigms and the languages that go with them (see Thomas S. Kuhn, *The Structure of Scientific Revolutions*). In contrast, we don't discard the anguish of a father bent over his dead daughter (King Lear), or a man making a Faustian pact with the bitch goddess Success to win back the love of a woman (Gatsby), and so on. Further, we don't discard the language that creates this stuff either. In the case of King Lear, the language that lets us see his magnificent ruin has outlasted Newtonian optics. Science deals with things, not human beings, and is speechless.

Fifty years ago Paul Tillich wrote, "It seems that the emphasis on the so-called 'empirical' method in theology has not grown out of actual theological demands but has been imposed on theology under the pressure of a 'methodological imperialism,' exercised by the pattern of natural sciences." Basically he says there's been a corruption of theology by the encroachment of scientific understanding into places where it doesn't belong. This "methodological monism," or the idea that a single system can describe everything, spreads out and in imperial fashion colonizes chemistry, theology, the study of literature and history, etc. But, he writes, "reality itself makes demands, and the method must follow; reality offers itself in different ways, and our cognitive intellect must receive it in different ways. An exclusive method applied to everything closes many ways of approach and impoverishes our vision of reality." You never want to forget that the encounter with life comes first; and an ascendant methodology, foreign to the subject in the first place, shouldn't stand in the way of that encounter.

"Our descriptions are better," Nietzsche wrote of older stages of knowledge and science, "but we do not explain any more than our predecessors."

To examine the description/explanation problem, let's look quickly at a column by Terry McDermott that ran in the *Seattle Times* on Sunday, November 16, 1997. Prefatorily: I have nothing good to say about this column. It was smug, it was mingy, it was a skimpy eight hundred words (Anna Karenina, in contrast to Letourneau, was given eight hundred pages before Tolstoy pitched her under a train) that hinged on a kind of fallacious reasoning that had by the day of sentencing become a staple of casual analysis, namely that if Letourneau had been a man and X a girl, we'd have no qualms about sentencing her to "four years in the joint."

Here's the song sung in rounds:

—Karil Klingbeil (director of social work, Harborview Medical Center): "I doubt that had there been a male perpetrator, it would have resulted in the same sentence."

—Nancy Grace (Court TV): "And let me guarantee you that if these roles were reversed and a male teacher had had sex with a 12- or 13-year-old student there would be no question that he'd be sent to jail."

—Shannon Peddycord (Bothell resident, in a letter to the *Times*): "Can you imagine had this been Joe-Stud Teacher and the victim a curvy 13-year-old girl?"

—And McDermott (in his column):

Mary Letourneau, 35, a schoolteacher, has an affair with a 13-year-old boy, a former student of hers.

The affair produces a guilty plea to charges of second-degree child rape. It also produces a baby and, last week, a suspended sentence.

Mark Blilie, 42, a schoolteacher, has an affair with a 15-year-old girl, a former student of his.

The affair produces a conviction for third-degree child rape and child molestation and four years in the joint for Blilie.

What's wrong with this?

I mean, other than the fact that both these people did horrible things, that they abused children and the hopes and trust of entire communities.

What's wrong, of course, is the similarity of the situations and the vastly different outcomes.

How did this happen?

The answers are . . ."

First off, "the joint"—I love that hard-boiled tough-guy lingo. When McDermott uses it the meaning is deceptive and suggests a real familiarity, not with prison or jails or the justice system, but with the genre of film noir and detective fiction, a filtrated and highly stylized knowledge of the underworld. Or maybe it was borrowed from the mouth of Frank Sinatra circa 1955. At any rate, as language the word just kind of hangs there, archaic and referential. *The joint*—never mind that it's antique slang, it's also about the most colorful and decorative word McDermott uses in the column and thus calls attention to itself, asking for examination. In the piece it functions rhetorically by setting up a crusty hardened term to contrast with the softness of Letourneau's heart and her weak and womanish insistence on love, *love* being a word presumably not used a whole lot in the mean dark weary bleak Bogey-haunted Sinatra-soundtracked inky black-and-white precincts McDermott inhabits down around Fairview Ave.—except maybe to describe a desperate broad or femme fatale or some other pathetic delusional female type. In the course of his column that softness of the heart, of her tendrilled hair, of a love that "mystifies everyone but her" is roundly dismissed, and McDermott's manly argot, the inner language of the knowing, is triumphant. Aided by this trope he concludes what everybody else concludes and does so by eliminating the mystifying element, love, from the equation.

"But when good people do bad things and do them on purpose, we are left without our normal, comforting rationalizations. It's very scary because in the end we are left to wonder: What about us?"

Thus ends the flow of rhetoric, on a note of pretend wonder. Tonally this piece took condescension to familiar heights for the *Seattle Times*. To begin, who exactly does that possessive include? It's my feeling McDermott's "our" refers, not to mine or yours, but to his and, by extension, the *Times*'s "normal, comforting rationalizations," and that with this statement he's entered metajournalistic territory, sort of embedding a ghostly self-reflexive footnote to himself about the nature of the newspaper business and its questionable ability to cover anything that isn't "normal," etc. What's "scary" here is the paper's brief venture outside its objective stance and into the mysterious and confusing moral universe, a place it probably doesn't belong. Put differently, the *Times*, with its protectorate sensibility, its wooden prose, and its stolid remove from the fray is really just trying to tidy up the universe in the image of itself. I can't tell, but it kind of seems to me from many readings of the final paragraph that McDermott's blaming Letourneau for failing to clarify herself into a cliché à la Veronica Lake, that he's accusing her of being beyond understanding, of not fitting his story, of eluding his dated language, of monkeying with his sense of the normal, the comforting, the rationalized. Ergo we get "scary." Withal the entire column is written in the storybook language and syntax of a Junior Scholastic reader, providing a universe of "good people" and "bad people," a world where things are "very scary" or a fuzzy warmth is evoked by acknowledging that in situations like this "the answers are as simple as human history, and as complicated as the human heart."

A sentence like that sounds awfully resonant but you have to wonder if the writer in laying down the words had anything real in mind beyond the creation of sound effects. Read the sentence more than once and the vaguely axiomatic philosophical construction, the balanced but weary knowledge of the world's ways, the parallel repetition of *human*, the apposing of *heart*

and *history*, might give you, as it did me, the sense of
a sentence whose meaning probably mystifies everyone
but the writer.

The easy interchangeability of the terms (if Letourneau were a man, X a girl) strikes me as a queer and
cruel exercise in abstract thinking that depends on a
mistake and a horrible forgetting. The mistake is to
confuse what's merely similar with what's equal—
"nothing is really equal" (Nietzsche)—and then pass it
off as logic. On even the superficial level there seem to
be plenty of differences between the two situations, but
on the existential level there is nothing but difference.
Letourneau and Mark Blilie are two different people,
not data, not exempla, not variables awaiting quantity
or value in a math equation. And this leads to the forgetting. What kind of damage is done to our ability to
love or understand and thus fully judge one another
when daily we're encouraged to forget that people are
people and view them instead as so much pasteboard,
scenery, clutter, generalized instances (of murder, of
rape, of embezzlement, etc.)? Here's a confounding
particular: from what I've been able to gather, the boy/
the child/the victim, X, is actually a couple of inches
taller than Letourneau. In terms of physical gifts alone
he's a young man. But this was never brought up in the
Times/Post-Intelligencer reportage, although it would,

it seems to me, slightly alter or maybe completely redo a reader's picture of the child/the boy/the victim. Certainly it would affect your understanding.

There is in the press that will toward allegory, that tendency to find the model in every situation, to treat the swiftly passing moments of a vivid and specific life as illustrations in a large, stable, highly abstracted story. But what if the case of Letourneau does not apply to you and me in any parabolic sense? What if it's singular and freakish? What if it's exceptional, elusive? Where do we turn if we want to fully understand life in this anomalous form?

"The sympathetic heart is broken," D. H. Lawrence wrote. "We stink in each other's nostrils." Perhaps this harsh assessment of the modern soul is true, but perhaps what's even truer, today, is that we no longer even smell each other. One Florence Wolfe (affiliated with an outfit called Northwest Treatment Associates) prefaced a televised discussion of "the situation" by claiming she "had no sympathy" for Letourneau. This struck me as a bizarre kind of prophylaxis. She was basically holding her nose. You can hardly explain anything without explaining the explanation and thus risking a regressive freefall, but here goes. "The great secret of morals is love; or a going out of our nature, and an identification," P. B. Shelley wrote. "A man, to be greatly good, must imagine intensely and comprehensively; he must put himself in the place of another and of many others. . . . The great instrument of moral good is the imagination." Just so I don't come across as a total poet-loving fruitcake (it's just that the interests of language were underrepresented in this case, that's why I keep bringing in these witnesses, these poets and novelists), Adam Smith—a free-market economist!—also helped make central the sympathetic identification that imagination allows us to extend to others. And Keats refined the idea further in his famous letter on negative capability, describing a state in which "man is capable of being in uncertainties, Mysteries, doubts."

(This is not to say that I think we'd be better off if these poets, these drunks, suicides, melancholiacs, queers, and ninnies were heads of state, only that they provide us the best record we have of the shifting sensitivities of language, the changes that in turn most carefully register movement in our evolving consciousness.)

At any rate, by the eighteenth or nineteenth century, imagination is seen as a pretty important epistemological faculty, and one of its key ingredients happens to be sympathy. This general idea hasn't entirely disappeared, despite various attacks, most of them non-philosophic-intellectual-academic and instead technological, economic, geographic—whatever, but still, it seems odd that an expert whom presumably we've turned to for insight announces as a kind of caveat that sympathy is going to be removed from the equation of her understanding. Other experts did the same thing, e.g., Patrick Gogerty from Childhaven, who was quoted postsentencing in the *Post-Intelligencer* as saying, "This is pure and simple exploitation of a child," when quite clearly there was nothing pure or simple about the situation, and the conditions (purity, simplicity) imposed on his point of view were just a framing device used to narrowly focus the idea of "exploitation" by excluding other, wider possibilities. This, *I* don't understand. Imagination, Wordsworth said, is amplitude of mind. But maybe sympathy's just a pain in the ass, maybe a sympathetic understanding would only muddy the works on television when all that's being asked for is a minute or two of high-cost clarity. Maybe a reasonable person understands you have to sacrifice certain things if you want your face on the small screen. And so in a devil's pact with the boob tube you unload your ballast of sympathy in order to deliver clarity, maintaining the *au fond* quality of your expertise, which is the providing of rock-solid and irrefutable and immobile answers. That is, you deliver ideas, insights, opinions, etc., as things. But why should I concede Florence Wolfe authority when it seems to me she's stated in advance that she plans to use only a limited perspective on the matter? She pulls out a pin and puts a prick in Wordsworth's amplitude of mind, deflating it just a little, and at that moment disqualifies herself, it seems to me, as someone to take seriously.

A few in-court observations.

First, the two psych experts, Dr. Moore for the defense and Dr. Wheeler for the prosecution. What interested me most about their respective turns on the stand were the props they used and how those props differed and perhaps reflected their positions more succinctly than either doctor's windy recondite testimony. Moore fixed a big paper tablet to an easel and, beginning significantly with a blank page, used a red felt pen to draw a diagram that continued for several flowing pages. The paper was wrinkled and rough and the doctor's hurried handwriting was illegible. Her diagram forked and forked again with hasty hypomanic enthusiasm and was almost instantly an incomprehensible madly branching maze, but the interesting thing was to watch her make it up, like Harold with his purple crayon, as she moved forward, flipping to new pages, new ideas, new possibilities. You never knew what might happen next.

Wheeler, by way of contrast, came to court with his chart already decided and drawn up, a one-page rectangular placard preprinted with blocky text and bulleted items. From where I sat in the cheap seats his chart looked like the last line in a doctor's eye examination and was also unreadable. In fact, I'm guessing no one in the courtroom could read either doctor's signs. It was kind of absurd. The easel angled away from both the bleacher full of journalists and the judge and was too far away for the rest of us to read and there was no jury that might need a visual aid to keep things straight, so what was the point? Moore's chaotic and bifurcating diagram captured and reflected her contentions about the bipolar state of Letourneau's mind and also created an image of liberty with its ever-forking and freely wandering path into the future; Wheeler's prearranged display offered a clear and orderly image of the future he was advocating for Letourneau, which was a clear sentence, a box, jail. While Moore's display moved through time, Wheeler's was static in time; hers evolved, his did not. Sitting there, you kind of wondered to what extent each doctor's chosen method of image-creation reflected not an understanding of Letourneau but an insight into their (the doctors') personalities; thus it also raised doubts about the solidity and objectivity of their science and their assessments of the case.

Second, I have to admit to large amounts of unpro-
fessional rock-butt and boredom, which I was able to
alleviate by occasionally shifting in my seat and closing
my eyes and listening to the sounds of people's voices.
But with my eyes closed I made a discovery. I heard
the prosecuting attorney speak in two distinct voices.
She used a sarcastic, dismissive voice while grilling Dr.
Moore and another, really irritating voice, hard to describe, but sort of storybook sorrowful, the kind of voice
you dip down into to read a tale's sad parts to a child,
when she was giving her summation. Now I come from
a pretty much jail-free family and none of us are lawyers
and so my courtroom experience, before that morning,
was nil. And attorneys I've seen in TV shows need to
convince me primarily as actors and only secondarily
as lawyers—the TV case, in other words, is decided on
good or bad drama, not law—so nothing had prepared
me for the bad acting, the transparent, awful acting, on
the part of the real-life prosecutor, Lisa Johnson. Especially during the summation, her voice tried to offer the
aural image of concern, of gravity, of direness, but it
was nowhere near the real thing itself. Her voice carried
no genuine conviction and came off as sentimental, at-
tempting to force on me, the listener, a feeling that was
not there, that wasn't earned. And while I understand
she's a lawyer, not an actor, still, that day, she played two

different characters in court and then a third outside, using three very different voices. There was the Sarcastic and the Sentimental and lastly the Press Conference voice, and I bring this up and think it's worth noting only because in contrast Letourneau, in all the taped interviews I watched and listened to, in all the stories I read, never feigned emotion, never once took on, even for effect, a false character.

Third, Letourneau was given a chance to speak, and did rise and say a few words and wanted to say a few more, but the press interrupted and all at once started shooting photos of her. Cameras clicked like locusts, making an amplified chewing sound. It was an unbelievably ugly, swinish, and rude moment, but so far as I know it's not been mentioned anywhere in the accounts of that day, a little omission about how Letourneau wanted to speak and was literally cut short and silenced by the media.

The law and the courts said Letourneau's crime was the rape of a child in the second degree. Shrinks for both the defense and the prosecution argued it was the sequela of a sickness, it was "hypomania" or a flaw in her "decision-making algorithm." Experts talked of abuse and rationalization and exploitation, pure and simple. Terry McDermott said it was just generically "scary." No one in or out of court bothered to bring in an ace authority on either love or language, so I'll do it myself, I'll swear in Gustave Flaubert, who wrote that "fullness of soul can sometimes overflow in utter vapidity of language, for none of us can ever express the exact measure of his needs or his thoughts or his sorrows; and human speech is like a cracked kettle on which we tap crude rhythms for bears to dance to, while we long to make music that will melt the stars."

Anyway, you could see the day of the sentencing, as experts in psychology and sociology and law summed up and asserted their positions, how language was being leveraged, how each fragmented field with its highly specific problem-solving vernacular was in a way carting off pieces of Letourneau, and how in the end there was nothing left of the very thing she had probably hoped would unify her shattered life, this elevated, fanatical, rule-exempt, healing notion of love. The courtroom side of things lasted less than three hours. Afterward there were clustered press conferences on the front lawn of the Regional Justice Center. Experts, specialists, lawyers and whatnot kept insisting—this, that, etc.—but the whole before/after aspect of the sentencing was lost on me because, following the judgment, nobody had anything new to say. ❖

Doo-Wop Down the Road:
Richard Brautigan

When Richard Brautigan shot himself in Bolinas in 1984, his life was given a loosely emblematic look that had very little to say about the literary value of his books. By then his obituary had been stalking him for some time: he was the broken and alcoholic hippie, the cultural figure of somewhat transient interest, the writer whose reputation rested on the drugged sensibilities of his contemporaries. It was as if the era itself had created a vogue for Brautigan no different from paisley shirts or Frye boots; he was treated as an embarrassing fashion. There are several reasons for this, not the least of which is a peculiar sort of shame. People who read Brautigan typically pick him up in high school or college, at a time when the lyrics to rock songs are still compelling, and a similar sensibility—youthful, I suppose—has always energized a reading of, for example, *Trout Fishing in America*. I don't really understand why this should be so, but both enthusiasms are hard to sustain past the age of thirty. We shoot our heroes and enjoy peripeteia as a spectacle akin to sport and perhaps harshly disavowing the past protects us from the disappointment of our outsized hopes—who knows, really, but shifts in taste don't fully account for the phenomenon. At any rate, nearly everything urgent and alive becomes doo-wop down the road, at least in this country's pop culture, and along the way a somewhat self-hating irony lays waste not only to the work but to the desires it once carried. It's like we die into adulthood.

"Always at the end of the words someone is dead," Brautigan wrote in one of his short stories, hitting the dark note of fear that haunts all his writing. But the obituaries for Richard Brautigan eulogized an era more than a man or his work. It's hard to go on admiring, and as a literary mode, the panegyric, drained of praise, is very common today. The web in particular is full of mock elegies that ridicule and are creepy in the way they so blithely break a fundamental promise, that we will take care of our dead. I suppose they are easy to pull off because the position of superiority is built in: there are the living, and then there are the dead, who are somehow at fault for dying, for letting time take them away. The right tone and rhetorical distance are lazily arrived at and almost second nature for someone raised in media culture. For example: Before he shot himself, Brautigan set the lights in his house to run on timers so that it would appear to the outside world as though he were still alive. One imagines him in those numb last hours plugging in lamps and, in a final fiction, re-creating the habits of the living, trying as he set the dials to remember what those rhythms were like. He was a depressive and something of a recluse and apparently his little gimmick worked. His neighbors left him alone. When he was found, weeks later, the manuscript he'd been editing, his last, penciled in blue, was partly eaten by maggots.

So much for his career.

Now only the prose remains, the cracked and cloddy prose with its black sad mood and shrugging *whatever* attitude, its pleonasms and curious grammatical lapses, its loopy metaphors that either strike home or fall so wide of the mark they read as an extremely flat deadpan. He read Faulkner all his life, obsessed with a past that would not pass, but the simple and often clunky sound of Brautigan's sentences is musically closer to Hemingway. Raymond Carver and Richard Brautigan shared the influences of time and place, as well as alcoholic fathers, rootlessness and poverty, and a love of fishing. They were contemporaries, born several years apart, both from the Northwest, and looking at old pictures of the men it would be easy to mistake them for brothers. In writing, the influences they shared show up most noticeably when you set Brautigan's work beside the stories Carver wrote in *What We Talk About When We Talk About Love*. Even the title of that collection borrows a crudeness from Brautigan, an inarticulate sloppiness, and the stories themselves, in their short inflected sentences, in their often surreal imagery, in their brevity and density and episodic plotting, in their characterizations and settings and dialogue, suggest a close affinity with *Revenge of the Lawn*, Brautigan's book of stories. Both books are quite voicey, they share a diction, and, even more noticeably, I think, the sentences find their sound and rhythm in speech that is, to my ear, regional.

Brautigan never wrote elegant prose. The sentences sound broken, physically broken, as if scrawled by a child with a stub of pencil and jabbed through the paper—they sound just slightly illegible, just slightly as though they hadn't earned a rightful place in the pages of a real book. They aren't fully enunciated. There's a loneliness in the sentences, they feel so untutored, so helpless—all of his work has the mood of a solitary child trying to amuse himself. I remember reading years ago a comment by Wallace Stegner, who claimed that Brautigan was illiterate, at least in the cultural sense. I rather doubt it, but a recurring figure in his work is the writer who should not be writing, the writer whose past is unusable and whose gifts are inadequate. "I'm haunted a little this evening by feelings that have no vocabulary. . . . I've been examining half-scraps of my childhood. They are pieces of distant life that have no form or meaning. They are things that just happened like lint."

By far the best of the stories on this theme is "1/3, 1/3, 1/3," which Carver included in *American Short Story Masterpieces*, an anthology, edited with Tom Jenks, that in some ways marks a high point for the flexible practice of realism in short fiction. In that story, three people are "going in" on the writing of a novel, and the narrator, who lives "in a cardboard-lined shack of [his] own building," has been included in the project because he owns a typewriter. A woman on welfare will do the editing because she's "read a lot of pocketbooks and the *Reader's Digest*." And the novelist is "writing the novel because he wanted to tell a story that had happened to him years before when he was working in the woods."

"You'll type it. I'll edit it. He'll write it," the woman says. They'll share the royalties, they agree.

None of the characters are given names, but the region is, acting as a sort of fourth character.

"I was about seventeen," the narrator says, "and made lonely and strange by that Pacific Northwest of so many years ago, that dark, rainy land of 1952. I'm thirty-one now and I still can't figure out what I meant by living the way I did in those days."

Really the antagonist in this story is the region. Brautigan always said he was from the Pacific Northwest, but it was rarely a place on a map. It was something ominous and waiting, a past that would not die off, that followed him everywhere. It was huge, it was vague. It was a weather, it was a sawmill and a pond and unpaved streets and puddles, it was a "ragged toothache sky" and a sad trailer "with a cemetery-like chimney" and children who sit in gutters like "slum sparrows." There's a sense throughout Brautigan's work that his metaphors and similes are reaching, that they're trying too hard, grasping after an effect in desperation. Often they succeed, but just as often they fail. What interests me is their staunch physicality, the yoking of terms, one abstract, the other concrete, that won't quite yield a just or decorous relation; they're like a landscape that won't give in to writing. Just breezing through some thoughts on the nature of metaphor provides a good way to understand Brautigan. If metaphor is meant to evoke new meanings—meanings not predetermined by either language or experience—then Brautigan's frequent attempts and failures are a stab at liberation in an already decided world. If metaphor depends on an eye for resemblances, then Brautigan's failures become fearful, a fear that nothing he knows resembles anything in the outside world, that everything is estranged and forever and obdurately strange. If metaphor is a transaction between words and things, then in Brautigan the deal is often torn up, the transaction called off.

Sometimes it seems as if his metaphors are trying to renew perception in a world that's overbearingly familiar. This is why his metaphors are so often either sly or ham-fisted, either timid or rudely "pounding at the gates of American literature." The place—as something physical, concrete—is resistant to new hopes. One of the terms in a typical Brautigan metaphor is always out of order; the human substance doesn't connect with the inhuman material. The closest I can come to understanding this is that somehow time is removed from the idea of place so that everything is eternally the same. The place doesn't change in either historical or seasonal time and gathers an oppressive weight because of it, always present, always an obstacle. The failed metaphors become a sign for this stern and inflexible relation. That people live in the region—unable to connect with it—is the real curiosity, the strange and baffling thing, and I think it's fair to say of Brautigan and his work that the place, this haunting Pacific Northwest, is like a father, and the broken little sentences are a spurned child afraid to speak up. Many of his characters never grow up; time is taken away from them, just as it is removed from the landscape. In "1/3, 1/3, 1/3," the woman is "so fragile and firmly indebted . . . that she often looked like a child twelve years old." Even the narrator is still seventeen, still slogging through the same wet streets, still living in the shack, unable to move forward in time—he can't figure it out. It's as if the land takes hold of the characters and won't let go. And if metaphor is partly meant to resist paraphrasis and reduction, pitting itself against the death of language, then Brautigan's failures make sense. I would say they are the soul of his writing, its chief draw. Failure is where his writing lives.

What's essential to Brautigan's life and work had so little to do with the sixties. The hippie California he moved to and became famous in was an outlandish trope for the future and a new society, but Brautigan was a solitary and his sentences were broken from the beginning and never found the sort of healing expansion Carver eventually arrived at. Carver's sentences discovered generosity and grew longer late in his career; Brautigan's didn't. One of the truths about suicide is that it's hardly ever about the future. It's the past the suicide can't face, and although disgrace appears to be the exception, the one instance where suicide seems to be about the future, even in *Oedipus*, it's her past Jocasta can't accept, once it's come to light. Brautigan never really left the Pacific Northwest, and all his sentences ever needed for completion was a death. ❖

Any Resemblance to Anyone Living

There's a fair chance I'll be on the best-seller list this season, not as a writer but as a character in someone else's fiction. It's supposed to be a secret, my true identity. I know I shouldn't talk about the book qua book—it's not seemly, I've been told—but I can't resist making a few general observations about what it feels like to find myself in a novel. Naturally I wonder where characters come from, and this particular angle, this perspective, the idea that someone might make use of me—of my hair, my clothes, my smell, my words, my little bundle of biographical facts—for material in a story is just too strange and juicy to pass up. Strictly speaking I'm the antagonist, or one of them, thwarting the heroine, and I appear in the book thinly, predictably disguised as a painter (meaning I'm moody, romantic, and dead broke). I've chopped up and rearranged a few people myself, making fiction. My poor motley father's appeared in my stories as a dead Vietnam vet, pill-addled insurance underwriter, mental patient, deranged mountaineer, and sentimental rapist—all this on top of having to live his regular life as . . . whatever. I can't help it. Every time my soul goes black I see his big hilarious grin. He's never said a single word to me about my writing, except to observe that it's bullshit. Deep down I'm sure he just doesn't dig the way he figures in my imagination, and in order to redress some of the distortions I've pushed into public, he's currently shopping a manuscript of his own, called *La Famiglia*. It's a trilogy! He has every right to hack out his own tale and set the record straight. I've read parts of what appeared to be the variorum edition of the book, replete with scholarly notes, annotations, emendations, furnished by the world's leading authority on my father—i.e., my father—and enjoyed it quite a bit. I hope he publishes it.

The book I'm in was written by an ex-love, and our shared experience is, I suppose, communal property. I don't come off badly as a character. The novel isn't some kind of slander or calumny or even the farrago of complaints you might imagine. Quite the opposite—on finishing a first read of the book I thought: I gave you better material than that! As a character I'm patient, gentle, and steady, I look good and I smell good, I'm intermittently wise, I don't ever act like the miserable broken bad animal that I was in real life. I was a monster! (Or perhaps not—is that possible? Was I decent, on occasion? I've got a weather-eye for misery but really don't see happiness or goodness as well as I should.) But forget life—in the book I've been Oprah-fied or Fabio-cated—altered, at any rate, but not really transformed. It's more like I've been redecorated. The cosmetic improvements feel like a neutering to me, but I believe the intent was to treat me gingerly, with circumspection, perhaps to flatter, perhaps to idealize. Still, the delicate conventions of romance have swept away some of the dirt and grit (also a convention, I'm sure) that I consider an essential part of my life. Elsewhere in the book I find myself quoted and (once again!) misunderstood, and there are bits of autobiography—one bit in particular that was tremendously painful and humiliating to me—that have been washed in soft soap to make the annoying narrator more likable. And then, here and there, my character is portrayed as yet another version of that man who gets mocked in sitcoms, a lumpy, obtuse, uncommunicative, clueless goofball. I get a little knocked around by the zeitgeist, a typical man, a wide target, an effigy stuffed with generic gripes. I'm a cliché! I probably deserve it—but does the book?

It's weird, the whole relation of fiction to fact. Recently I gave a reading in Seattle. A woman I've taught came up to talk about whatever, and started in, eventually, about a couple of my recent stories. She said, how can I read you (Me? Not the work?) the same now that we have a history? A history? I've always thought of this woman as a stalker. I like her, but she patronizes me, and whenever I see her at a public event she's always sighing sadly and tolerantly, as if she alone possesses a special wisdom about me or the situation. It's like she's watching me with great pity as I'm being hauled off to some kind of doom I can't really comprehend. It gives me the creeps. And she feels completely free to touch me in public—that night she reached right in and straightened the collar on my coat, so, she said, I'd look good for my "adoring fans." Huh? Later I was told, by her friend, that this woman said she was able to spot me from across the crowded basement at Elliott Bay merely by seeing my knees. My knees are bulky knobs of bone like everybody else's, and I was wearing my usual attire of droopy brown corduroys, plus if my dress code has any animating principle whatsoever it's anonymity. When it comes to clothes I've always been a frightened boy, opting, as we do, for bulk and dullness and colors of the sort the world fades to when left alone—I build in a little neglect in advance of real abandonment.

She brought up typewriters. I'd published a story about a typewriter repairman and his schizoid son. To me the story was a vague attempt to create a world in which love between men wasn't laughable. I was so sad about this problem—it descended on me, a pure mood, a scary hollow—that I had to write in order not to feel totally bereft. I was desperate and obsessed in the writing because I needed to believe that that world of love really might exist, if not for me, somewhere, for someone. Now, this stalker-woman had once given me a lovely old Underwood that, beautiful as the machine was, I felt highly ambivalent about accepting. I sensed I was agreeing to something unstated, that I was obligating myself, that I was making a swap. We both know the place that was one of the models for the repair shop in my story, although I'd actually set the business on another street in Seattle, mostly because the real street is boring and my make-believe street has a better view of the water. But to this woman, I think, the story was about the real shop and the real guy and, I fear, some sly, public acknowledgment, on my part, of our private shared interest in old manual typewriters. It was as if the story were a tryst we'd had, some clandestine rendezvous. I always feel like that woman is making a fiction out of me.

But how do I feel about being turned into a character in an actual novel? I've been asking people, just casually, if there are any ethics about this kind of thing, and happily most people say there aren't. I agree. For a lot of people who write there's an unspoken, prior silence that feels nearly conspiratorial; a heavy suggestion that you don't tell the truth, don't mention the drunk father, the cold mother, the rapist next door, the molester at church, the sorrow and despair of even a thing as small and forgettable as a Sunday afternoon; some pressure against saying out loud what's obvious. Sometimes we literally make a pact—don't tell!—but more often shame or confusion or a profound dislocating pain does the work of swearing us in. We keep secrets and hold to silence because what's obvious is overwhelming, it's baffling and mysterious. The very surface of life makes the sinister suggestion, and that's one of the reasons the best writers I know are fascinated by the ordinary—it's so shockingly alive with trouble. When you deny the surface, then the impulse to write prose dies, I think, and I'm with Bellow's Augie March on this, that there's no fineness or accuracy of suppression, that by holding down one thing you hold down the adjoining. If I believe that for myself, I've got to believe it for others too.

In part owing to its epistolary form there's not much *Bovary, c'est moi* in the book, and my character in particular isn't the sort that emerges from contradictions deep inside the author's soul. I'm there in a chunky undigested way. I kind of hang out in the novel like a big dope. Real life weighs down my character, I think, and he never achieves autonomy, any meaningful freedom from the facts. In an interview with the *Paris Review*, Graham Greene said, "One never knows enough about characters in real life to put them into novels. One gets started and then, suddenly, one can not remember what toothpaste they use . . . and one is stuck utterly. No, major characters emerge; minor ones may be photographed." I'm photographed—and yet at the same time, stuck in a vague real-life fidelity, my character seems sociological, his presence in the book determined by the demands of genre, a phenomenon coughed up by the culture at large. These things aren't contradictory. A novel in letters is naturally apostrophic, addressing absent persons, and my character feels absent to the point of vacancy. He has no inner life and hence no conflicts or desires of his own. I think he's supposed to be a big character but in fact he has a minor feel, always walking in the door at the right moment, a creaky mechanism servicing the needs of a melodrama. Writers generally pay for their melodrama by resorting to types, in essence turning all their characters, in Forster's formulation, flat. My character is the dullest part of an otherwise lively story. He's there because I was there in life, but life is a bad reason for including a character in a story. The book would have been way better had he been cut from it.

There's no factory that turns life into fiction, no machine for digging up good raw material and stamping out stories. Anyone who's taught creative writing has heard the excuse "But this really happened" as a way to justify the most implausible events. A lot of readers, however, want to smelt fiction in order to separate the truth from the slag, not the uppercase sort of Truth but the humdrum kind that conforms to facts, to actuality. At readings people often ask what part of a story is true, as if assaying its value, the idea being that the fictional element is an alloy, an impurity that debases real events. The general preference is for naïve readings, I've found, where authenticity is measured or verified or defined by facts—the writer's bio says he was an acrobat, and the main character in his novel is, it turns out, an acrobat. I tend to see everything written as some form of fiction, more or less convincing. Still, the urge to resolve the fiction into something irreducible—real life, the genuine article—doesn't go away. I've talked to students about that typewriter story and inevitably the question comes up, phrased more or less like this: Where do you get your inspiration? I know what they want to hear, and I give it to them: My brother is schizophrenic. But I'm quick to add that the story isn't about my brother, that it comes from somewhere else and goes off to its own, individual destiny. I do have a good ear for crazy talk because I've listened to gobs of it. I have a feel for the loneliness of loving a mentally ill person who can never really return that love. I'm a fan of old typewriters and, for Christmas, was just given my best machine ever, a classic Olivetti Valentine, designed by the great Ettore Sottsass. So that story has typewriters and rain, Seattle streets and schizophrenics, Catholicism and donuts and city buses and social workers—stuff I know about—but it isn't about me or my brother or anyone I could call on the phone.

Certain images presided over the writing—of a wall of typewriters, each with a blank white sheet of bond rolled in the platen, an image that haunted me like a dream for three years before I wrote the story; of a man in a worn blue smock hunched at his bench while his grown son says the rosary, and particularly the silence between them, the invasion of small sounds, of the tools, the glass beads, the rain against the window; of the love that exists in old objects, and how those objects, loved over time, might teach an otherwise inarticulate man to be steady and strong and loving toward all broken things, including his son. Perhaps that's what the story is about. Or perhaps it's about the technical challenges, the difficulty of writing "I love you" so that it isn't ironic or disgusting or a pathetic joke; of using crazy dialogue in a way that feels just right—without condescension or sentimentality—and therefore in some way makes a legitimate home for the voice of a mentally ill man; of capturing the sound of the sentences, a sound that isn't precious, by eliminating, as much as possible, the emotional fussiness of commas—instead using hard consonants and the natural stresses of our largely iambic language to create the rhythm. I was in a phase of full-blown anti-comma mania as I wrote, believing robust American prose could be written with hardly any punctuation. The man I was writing about was a practical man, a man whose life wouldn't admit many clauses or qualifications, many refinements—he would see his life as one headlong statement, without pauses or the luxury of separations or second thoughts, lacking a certain inwardness, and I wanted that rhythm in the story. That's the most autobiographical part of the story, this whole silly personal drama about punctuation.

When the writer first sent me a manuscript of the novel I kept marginal notes as I read, objecting to passages, characterizations, factual discrepancies. Your father wasn't like that, your mother, your sister, your brother, etc. Or: This never happened, that's not quite accurate, what about when, etc. Partway through the book I gave up, realizing I was arguing raw material, debating the very nature of life itself, fighting against history, memory, language, failed love, death, faith, everything. I felt claustrophobic, suffocated, having at that old life, those dead arguments. I really didn't like the book as an experience, but I wasn't sure how to say that, because . . . just because, let's say. In the end I gave her some notes that I thought were pretty balanced and sane but probably were not. When I received a signed copy of the book a few months later, I wasn't sure what to do with it. I put it on the kitchen table, set it on the floor, took it across the yard to my writing shed and stuck it on the bookshelf, brought it back to the house, held it, stared at it, then finally carried it out to the shed again, where it sat for a while, behind me, on an old gray typing table. But it was giving the room bad juju and I could feel a knot building between my shoulder blades as I worked. I stopped writing and took half a milligram of lorazepam and right about the time the benzo softened my bad mood, I picked up the book again and found my name—my real, actual name—in the acknowledgments, where the writer thanked me for being a great reader and a true friend. ❖

Degrees of Gray in Philipsburg
by Richard Hugo

You might come here Sunday on a whim.
Say your life broke down. The last good kiss
you had was years ago. You walk these streets
laid out by the insane, past hotels
that didn't last, bars that did, the tortured try
of local drivers to accelerate their lives.
Only churches are kept up. The jail
turned 70 this year. The only prisoner
is always in, not knowing what he's done.

The principal supporting business now
is rage. Hatred of the various grays
the mountain sends, hatred of the mill,
The Silver Bill repeal, the best liked girls
who leave each year for Butte. One good
restaurant and bars can't wipe the boredom out.
The 1907 boom, eight going silver mines,
a dance floor built on springs—
all memory resolves itself in gaze,
in panoramic green you know the cattle eat
or two stacks high above the town,
two dead kilns, the huge mill in collapse
for fifty years that won't fall finally down.

Isn't this your life? That ancient kiss
still burning out your eyes? Isn't this defeat
so accurate, the church bell simply seems
a pure announcement: ring and no one comes?
Don't empty houses ring? Are magnesium
and scorn sufficient to support a town,
not just Philipsburg, but towns
of towering blondes, good jazz and booze
the world will never let you have
until the town you came from dies inside?

Say no to yourself. The old man, twenty
when the jail was built, still laughs
although his lips collapse. Someday soon,
he says, I'll go to sleep and not wake up.
You tell him no. You're talking to yourself.
The car that brought you here still runs.
The money you buy lunch with,
no matter where it's mined, is silver
and the girl who serves your food
is slender and her red hair lights the wall.

Degrees of Gray in Philipsburg

The streets of Philipsburg do indeed seem laid out by the insane. Beyond West Broadway pavement gives out, and from then on the roads and streets are a seasonal affair, running with mud or bleached by dust or silent under new snow. Many of the streets that cut through town barely qualify as such; they are paths beaten in the grass, two tracks where trucks lurch over rocks with a clatter of bad linkage, roads of gravel or red cinder that skirt empty pastures and a few last houses until they head, somewhat pointlessly now, into the hills and mountains where men once worked. One can imagine many things about these evocative streets, and in some ways that's all that remains, imagination haunting a town where even history, usually the last to leave, has given up and gone away. One can imagine, for instance, that the roads are the ripped seams of a civilization, rents in the fabric that have led to a general unraveling, to the vacant storefronts and faded signs and a rusting school bus, still yellow, inexplicably parked in front of a hotel whose last guest signed his name to the register, one vanished afternoon, years ago. Perhaps the bus died there, the children walked to school that morning, and it was convenient and reasonable—since weeds had already grown up around the red brick steps and the windows were gone and the hotel, it was agreed, by some vague assent, was never coming back—to leave the bus where it was, like the carcass of a whale washed to shore. Time would take care of it, as it had the hotel. Now the bus has no windows, and who knows what became of the children. You don't see many of them on the streets of Philipsburg.

One can imagine the roads—somehow the word *streets* implies too much, is too elaborate—as the relics of haste and ambition, of a boom in silver that lasted a few short years, until the Repeal—and that word, *repeal,* seems fitting for a town whose future was never in its own hands—disrupted the hurried energy, and in fact crimped the flow of time generally. Houses had been flung up on the hillsides, and there was some need to connect them, but the original roads were probably platted by the tramping of tired men. That weariness, that exhaustion, is inscribed in the roads to this day. Things of course changed, but in some ways time reversed direction and began running backward, seeking the past as water does low level. But nostalgia, where loss finds rest, hasn't really taken root. Philipsburg's rival from the boom era, Granite, several miles back in the woods, higher and colder and more remote, is a ghost town now, the last resident, holding out as he worked a small claim, having died seventy years ago. You can walk *those* streets and still find the infirmary and the bank vault and the music hall and, pointedly, down a gully, the obligatory red-light district that always seems to follow wherever the work men do is an insult to their bodies. Presently someone is trying to rebuild the town, hoping to attract tourists, and on most Sundays in the summer, a few desultory visitors wander with a photocopied map through stands of stunted pine, looking, somewhat puzzled, at walls of leaning brick or the fairly intact stone house of the superintendent. Some of the shacks where miners lived still have their sad beds shoved into a corner, although those shacks are so small they seem to be made up solely of corners. A black stove, a chair by the window, and the space is filled. The size of these clapboard shanties doesn't suggest children, and it's as if the future, even from the beginning, was something you would have to establish in another town. The past was Granite's destiny from day one, and when the mines shut down for good, what was left of that past was packed up and moved in carts three miles down the mountain, settling in Philipsburg.

Entitling a poem or story or essay is harder than naming a child. The privilege of place is almost like a law of primogeniture, with the title inheriting the entire work, and along with that legacy comes the burden, the implied promise, of carrying the weight of the piece to the end. You want to avoid the didactic as well as a too vaguely allusive reference that will read portentously. Joyce named things well—"The Dead," *A Portrait of the Artist as a Young Man, Ulysses*—suggesting by example that simplicity and a certain cool aim at the center of a work is the way to go. Hugo's title goes that way, and yet I've always liked it, in part, because shadings of gray refer to weather, and weather is mentioned only once, obliquely, in a line of the poem where, even then, the accent falls on another word. This seems characteristic of a poet who is both blunt and self-effacing: the poem avoids wallowing in its most obvious mood. But while we're promised degrees of gray, like a chromatic study in painting, we descend through the poem, down through the broken self and ruined history and a stanza of questions with no satisfying answers, until we arrive at the final lines, in which, suddenly, a slender girl's red hair lights the wall. To a point, in other words, where the color red is the hero of the poem. Hugo is an honest writer, and his title is honest, I believe, but the light and youth and especially the vivid red, discovered down at the bottom of everything, is the one note in the poem that has always put me in a questioning, objecting state of mind. I've always felt—just vaguely, like a hitch in my reading—that Hugo pulled the red out of his hat.

After the onslaught of loss, both personal and historical, do we really believe a good lunch and an aesthetic perception settles the matter? Does red (and, by inference, poetry) save? Quite possibly poetry salvages nothing except language itself, and even that project of reclamation is up against poor odds. Poetry is not a social program and it's not easily accessible to everyone, despite its ancient mnemonic role and the currency of certain opinions by primitivists of the New Age. Nor is poetry liturgical, composed of sacramental language and containing a central mystery that can be approached, shared, and repeated, then made portable and evangelized and kept alive through ritual until its power rivals governments. The Pauline hopes of poetry recur now and then—in Shelley or Brodsky, for instance, or Edward Hirsch—but they don't result in many converts. Reading poems remains a cult practice of the few, and it's hard to imagine an art form further in temper from the reality of Philipsburg. Hugo's red might be epiphanic and passing, one of those visions we expect a poet to access, an insight confirming our solitude rather than rescuing us from it, but if this is so, does he really touch the ruin so richly itemized in the rest of the poem? Hugo's no aesthete, and he means for this red to be a real outcome, an inevitable result of looking directly at the degrees of gray. Because he's a poet, we have to take him at his word. Hugo says there's salvation in poetry, a saving, moreover, discovered at the bottom of ruin, and he's also suggesting, I think, that you must fall to find it.

I don't want to bog down in the exegetical rigging of real criticism, the cumbersome quoting, the whole vast tackle of arcane and specialized language that takes poetry further toward silence. Hugo's poem doesn't require it. It's written in free verse, sprung from the inner clock that keeps time in metrical poetry, and so the lines read like regular sentences, denser but not all that different from the ones in a daily newspaper. The poem's not fragile. You can beat on it. It's got good traction. Paraphrased, its four stanzas go like this:

1. You're fucked.
2. We're all fucked.
3. Why?
4. Let's eat lunch.

It isn't easy to say your life broke down. It isn't easy to say in conversation and expect anyone to listen, and it's desperately hard to say in poetry or prose and expect anyone to read. From my own experience I know the result, most of the time, is laughable. On a personal level, the problem seems to be that we know these things happen, but we don't ultimately know why they do, and anyone who steps forward too ready with phrases from pop psychology or offering details from personal history is either missing the deeper point or airing gripes. The problem for the poet is one of expression; nothing is quite so false, in writing, as the heartfelt confession. Irony in its least waggish form, scrubbed of cynicism, is necessary—a certain cool, a distance, the slight masking that occurs whenever the writer separates from his subject. Hugo's solution is to go for blunt, and most of this poem trades in symbols that batter the obvious, from broken-down cars to crazy streets to churches and jails and a prisoner, not knowing what he's done, who stands in for the state of the soul. The symbolism here is too much in the public domain, too shared for this to be a private excursion. Even if you wanted to, you couldn't wring a proprietary solitude from it. When Hugo says your life broke down, that's either metonymy or synecdoche, but we get the point, that its absent term is a car, and we accept it because of the banged-up humor and his refusal to be pretty about it. The directness is disarming, and it serves the subject—even our most durable, readily available solutions have failed. These symbols create a loneliness and isolation because their communal function has failed, but we still recognize their ghostly hopes as our own. In a single stanza Hugo sweeps up the whole of Western civilization. There are plenty of mouths, but the kiss that really eludes us is the good one—*failed love*. The streets are nuts, they either don't go anywhere or, if they do, all the destinations are dead ends—*failed thought*. Churches are kept up, but a church qua building is only a maintenance problem, no longer in the business of salvation—*failed spirit*. The hotels haven't lasted, and the jail's already lived out its Biblical allotment of years—*failed alibi, law*. You're a wreck, but you've come to a place that's an even worse mess—*failed individual, society*.

The auxiliary verb *might* subtly, brilliantly alters the universe, so that the *you* is not the poet addressing himself, or not strictly. If, instead, Hugo writes: You *came* here Sunday . . . then we're into confining facts, confessional accounts, moving a step away from the poem as written, with its broad, inclusive *you*, toward the self as a dead end, seeking private salvations. The *you* would then become the poet or a character standing in for the poet, and in any case, whatever hope or possibility the poem holds would be bracketed by the past tense, framed inside personal history, absorbed into a character whose formation was completed some time ago—into a world, in other words, that occurred, once and for all, prior to the poem. The perfect past would isolate the poet from his poem, quarantining the ruin to a time and place that's already been safely escaped; the poem would be the artifact left behind by an experience, losing an element of risk. Using the auxiliary *might* shifts the tone. We enter the poem through supposition, and are given, like an allowance, a small sum of uncertainty, to spend wisely or foolishly. By rescuing the first line from a finished past tense, *might* hints at a future, particularly in the sense that anything unknown belongs to an expectant time. It plants a seed of probability or possibility, even advisability. The word's brassy note rings like a harmonic, its long vowel sound finally flicking light against the wall. But how do we get there?

In this first stanza, the lines are typically short and flat, somewhat immobile, and the one line that departs from the pattern, the longest and most fluent, is about movement, particularly walking and acceleration. It's as if the poem panics inside its contracted space. Pathetically, it wants to go somewhere. The syntax is an echo of the sense, and there's fear and alarm in the sentence, a struggle between understanding and action, capturing a moment of awareness and the ensuing paralysis, when flight is the right impulse but the urge has atrophied and there really isn't anywhere to go. Each hurried clause is like a frightened, fading footstep. And then the urge dies, the brief flight stops, and the sentences, abrupt as walls, return to their immobility. The prisoner is always in—a curious phrase, in that he doesn't seem to be held against his will. He doesn't need to be. Awareness is gone, and with it, freedom. His imprisonment is a condition. He's bound to a cell by "not knowing," which isn't a defect of mind, but of comprehension, one we all share regardless of native gifts. That the prisoner lacks understanding might serve as a legal argument for his innocence, but no ruling, for or against, will release him from history.

Philipsburg is located in the Flint Valley, a valley so open and wide all movement along the highway feels annulled, and on the morning of September 11 nothing here changed. The vast space seemed to cancel out even conversation, and there was no rush to talk about the attack in New York. I'm not now inclined to fill this silence with supposition, to hazard guesses about the particular quality of the quiet in Philipsburg, except to say I felt it myself. While I can imagine people in New York or Boston or Omaha stunned by fear and outrage, that wasn't my situation, and I remember standing outside that morning, looking across the valley where already, in the higher elevations, snow had fallen, and feeling nothing, not horror or disgust, not shock or anger. A branch snapped by a surprising June snow, a dry hummock up the hill where fox denned in winter, these things held my attention, standing out, strange and real, in the nearby world. It may be true that we are ultimately saved from total loss, as Czesław Miłosz has written, because there's nothing to do but stare at the green leaf fluttering in the wind. Much of the news, as a form of expression, made little sense to me. People were saying our lives would never be the same again, a phrase turning naïvely around a moment that space, which is heartless, and nature, which is indifferent, would never share. Not even history agrees, and part of what made discussion so difficult was the intrusion of the historical into a romance, a confusion of genres we find particularly galling. Hawthorne called romance "a legend prolonging itself," whose hostile enemy is contact with history. Without any real conscious intention, I would find myself seeking a sense of that contact, turning to the work of Miłosz and Joseph Brodsky, writers who, knowing firsthand the horror of history, struggled between silence and noise to make their poems. But before that, days, a week after the attack, as voices emerged, as newscasters spoke, as opinions were aired, with noise becoming the norm, I found a photograph of a falling man that seemed to restore a necessary silence, and I pinned a copy to my wall. It seemed to me a place to begin, the only place.

Whereas prison, well, what is it, really? A shortage
of space compensated for by an excess of time.

—Joseph Brodsky

1.) The only prisoner; you're
fucked.

Brodsky's equation is just, I think, but you can tin-
ker with the terms and arrive at other prisons, other
compensations. This picture also brings us to a prison,
one without a shortage of space; in fact, there's a sud-
den, horrifying excess, a terrible liberation, with time
in short supply.

In this moment the falling man's time on earth is
a spatial concern, and he has more in common with
a stapler than he does with you or me. Natural laws
explain why he's dropping, and a formula can easily calculate the rate of his descent. A man of roughly that
weight, from roughly that height, in that specific gravity, arms and legs spread, reaches a terminal velocity of
125 mph, beyond which there's no further acceleration. Terminal velocity—of the man, a stapler, a rain-
drop—is the square root of $[(2 \times W) / (Cd \times r \times A)]$.[1]
That's the irresolvable contradiction in this picture, a
man subject to mechanistic forces, a life obedient to

---

1 Where W = weight, Cd = drag coefficient, r = density, and A =
frontal area.

335

an indifference—although *obedient* is a somewhat dead metaphor here, since rebellion or refusal is impossible. One might wonder if he jumped or not, a last act of volition, a final insistence on self, but either way falling is the consequence. In falling, he's lost connection, he's ripped free from every relation, to his love and work and family, to his own biography, to the choice he made that morning about what shirt to wear. The descent strips him of every cherished thing, even our regard, and one thinks of Auden's Old Masters who understood the position of human suffering, "how it takes place/While someone else is eating or opening a window or just walking dully along," and the amazing boy from Breughel, falling out of the sky, seen by a ship that "had somewhere to get to and sailed calmly on." The falling man is falling because that's what things do, and in some awful way it's not remarkable.

Just the same, there's an abstract purity to the picture, in the geometry of sky and building, that strangely suspends the man in a constructed space, entirely drained of time, so that one imagines him there forever. The composition is immaculate, even icily harmonious. In the picture's arrested moment you get a pure feel for the falling man's incomprehension, his emptiness, but in the days following the attack, obviously, this sensation would become intolerable to survivors, to the witnesses we were turned into, and the point of view would shift, the images would progress. Something was needed to distinguish the falling man from a fluttering scrap of paper, from the nothing of his silent descent. The pristine space began to blow with dust and fill with debris. Attention was focused on the broken hierarchy, the jumbled ruin. An accessible idea of heroism, Homeric but not tragic, occupied the human void, and suddenly firemen loomed up and moved across the foreground of the new images. "The savagery of the struggle for existence," Miłosz has written, "is not averted in civilization," and now we knew this, possibly. But a hasty gloss of evolution from primitive to modern was improvised, phoenixlike, out of the ashes, and contra the terrorists, who seemed to have reduced a symbol of at least one kind of civilized aspiration to a barbaric rubble. Rebuilding began in a rudimental, dark, superstitious state where blind luck or chance either saved or did not save. Later, it turned out that God was with the people who survived and the people who perished were now with God, a tautological tidiness that always breaks my heart, tearing at an old longing for universal justice. Faces were shown, names mentioned, chronologies elaborated, stories told, helping to rehabilitate the present scene, applying a patch to the moral sense. An ideal *civitas* emerged, so that, looking into the shadowy precincts of Wall Street, where certainly some of the dead were embezzlers, no mention was made of precisely the sort of intrigants who would, later, populate stories about Enron. It's almost too obvious to state, but in a random sample of any three thousand people, some will be beating their children, others will be addicted to heroin, and others still will be caught in the midst of affairs that would, left to run their course, damage families and undo to some degree the social fabric. But this was a new polis—from which those folks were now symbolically banished. Sincerity worked like a conduit for connection. What might have been viewed as a great equalizer, falling on the just and unjust alike, visited on the rich and the poor, the fair and the homely, black and white, instead rose out of the wreckage with a perfectly familiar face, looking quite the same as life before. Hierarchy was restored, and hatred with it. Enemies were declared, war was in the offing, and now the falling man, not knowing what he'd done, was descending through—or perhaps into—the medium of history, which sits between all of us and oblivion.

the premise supporting business

There has been considerable reflection on the origins of the phenomenon known as individualism, on Byronic despair—the revolt of the individual who considers himself the center of all

338

things, and their sole judge. No doubt, it was the contents of the imagination itself which forced this to happen, *as soon as hierarchical space began to somersault.* Anyone who looks into himself can reproduce the course of the crisis. The imagination will not tolerate dispersal and chaos, without maintaining one Place to which all others are related, and, when confronted with an infinity of relationships, always relative only to each other, it seizes upon its sole support, the ego. So why not think of myself as an ideal, incorporeal observer *suspended above the turning earth?* [Italics mine.]

—Czesław Miłosz

Hatred organizes space—think of Dante's *Inferno,* the structure of which is partly animated by personal enmity—and in the gray waste of the Philipsburg in Hugo's poem, it's the principal supporting business. The contracted, hating ego restores hierarchy, creating an armature for the emotions, organizing a defense of the inner life while it's attacked from outside. But hate and rage are emotions we summon to survive a crisis, and the acute phase can't be sustained for long. The adrenal medulla can't hack it. The surge of epinephrine is meant to peak and subside and pass entirely with the passing of the injury or threat. Without relief the nerves blunt, and even if the emergency remains, a numbing settles in obdurately; and that's the harmed, sinking, downward passage, from hatred to boredom, captured in the second stanza of the poem. Hugo moves in a quick line or two from rage and hatred to boredom, and I think he's right to push the association. Here, the hatred is against history, the mere unfolding of life, its indifferent or brutal or oblivious progress, against which the spiked rage can't strike out. It's a grievance against ghosts, a grievance against what's gone—or even, more accurately, against the sheer "going" of life everyone suffers. No wonder that in these ruined Western towns you so often find revivals along the lines of Hawthorne's legend prolonging itself, the sorry romance of the spurned, yearning to occupy the dramatic center once more by suspending time. The main drag in Philipsburg is either ruined or vacant or shabby or somewhat tartly gussied up, but these are all guises of the same settled arrangement, the same hierarchy. Hatred's destination is boredom, and boredom is perhaps a rebellion against time; it's the finished putting up a fight with the end. Boredom is, at any rate, a more habitable space, long-term, than history.

The British psychologist Adam Phillips calls boredom "that most absurd and paradoxical wish, the wish for a desire," and defined as such, boredom isn't fixed by distraction, by bars or restaurants, but by the arrival of a feeling of anticipation. I know for myself boredom involves a spatialization of time; the forwardness goes out of life, and I wait, and in waiting time becomes a place—not a particularly good one, but a place nonetheless, with the minutes and hours, the days and months piling up indifferently. For phenomenologists, this kind of repetition isn't a property of time but of space, and then it's more aptly called "redundancy," when things exceed what's necessary. In boredom you take on some of the character of an object, becoming lifeless and inanimate, lacking flow, and the more the time sense is rendered into space, the more isolated you become—isolated by becoming extraneous. The spooky intimation behind boredom, the whispered secret of it, is death, a final draining of time, when at last all the living belong exclusively to space. In boredom, we become victims of a sameness within a hierarchy whose original principle of design was a now-forgotten, vestigial loss of proportion—which is an aesthetic problem, the problem of arranging parts harmoniously within a whole.

What is worse, time, always strongly spatial, has increased its spatiality; it has stretched infinitely back out behind us, infinitely forward into the future toward which our faces are turned. . . . Today I cannot deny that in the background of all my thinking there is the image of the "chain of development"—of gaseous nebulae condensing into liquids and solid bodies, a molecule of life-begetting acid, species, civilizations succeeding each other in turn, segment added to segment, on a scale which reduces me to a particle.

—Czesław Miłosz

When hit by boredom, go for it. Let yourself be crushed by it, *submerge, hit bottom.* In general, with things unpleasant, the rule is, the sooner you hit bottom, the faster you surface. [Italics mine.]

—Joseph Brodsky

To fall and hit bottom life has to give up its hold on the horizontal, its restriction to the same level in a now-tedious hierarchy. For this, there's no choice but to descend, if only because hatred, that forgotten structure inside boredom, has already failed in its attempt to rise above history and circumstance. Upward progress is a social or economic idea, but from literature and, to an extent, religion, we know going down holds a lot of life's interesting possibilities. If up isn't an option, then down is the obvious alternative; it's even desirable. Down is the direction poetry travels on the page, anyway, and poets have tended to follow their pens. For contrast, the etymology of the word *prose* means to go forward, generally straight forward, and there's nothing internal to a sentence that limits its length or sideways nature. Paragraphing arranges ideas logically, but for that one could imagine a codex like an accordion, the folds expanding laterally. Even punctuation isn't really about organizing or shaping the inherently horizontal character of prose. Periods, commas, and colons regulate the breath, and well-written prose always includes, in its long or short rhythms, a kind of pulmonary function; reaching into these vital rhythms, good prose can, like breathing exercises in yoga, inhabit the visceral life of a reader. Conceivably prose could be written on ribbons hundreds of yards long, winding the reader and testing his lungs in another way, but we bind and store it in books, mainly, so that doesn't happen. The quotidian tendency of prose is either to satisfy an immediate disposable need or to point beyond itself, toward a distant, receding horizon of information. It's the *écriture* of choice for assembling bicycles and analyzing wars, and the difficulty for a writer, the danger, is that his words, failing to capture a cadent, living pulse, will lose meaning in the vastness of other words. If a piece of prose aspires to art, it must close itself off, setting in motion sympathetic vibrations and gaining, as with any enclosure, resonance.

Poetry's orientation is not primarily horizontal but vertical. It goes across, left to right, but mostly it goes down, top to bottom, and that descent is dictated from within. Though our language for prosody has largely shifted to a discussion of stresses, we still listen for feet and measure in meter the distance a line travels. The syllables in a haiku might be the exception to this idea of poetry's descent, but you'd lose the stillness in space if all seventeen were strung like clothesline across the page. While a haiku hangs, suspended in air, hexameter hits its beats and heads down, line by line, and it's easy to imagine an idea of descent and depth coming to a stymied poet by simply staring disconsolately at the page. The etymology of verse means "to turn" or "return," and if the trick in prose is to overcome its diffuse and vague and ubiquitous presence, the trap for poetry is hermeticism, its tendency toward the occult, the ease with which it turns in on itself and, going down, abandons or forfeits its participation in the upper world. Still, poetry has no choice about its generally chthonic direction. Even a democratic poet like

Whitman, resisting hierarchy's vertical axis with his broad, barbaric yawp, eventually descends. Down is where poetry is, and whatever poetry has to say, whatever it can deliver, is down there too.

In a trope typical of him, at least in this poem, Hugo monkeys with the expected syntactical arrangement, wrenching new emphasis from fairly accessible language; playing with inflection is a way he has of torquing a phrase, and he does it twice in the second stanza. Let me look at the second instance first. The mill "in collapse / for fifty years that won't *fall finally down*" gives us the adverb in its most active form. *Finally* doesn't idle in an ancillary place, taking up slack because the right verb wasn't available. In fact, for a word without a verbal form (except the somewhat bureaucratic *finalize*), *finally*, as Hugo writes it, is as close as you're going to get to a sense of the desire inside the downward trajectory of falling. Somehow the *down* here, the collapse, is being propped up, penultimately supported by an old, useless structure, and *finally* is the hope or possibility of falling, the fulfillment of fifty years of need. Positioned just above a stanza composed entirely of questions, the line suggests that the mill, slumped in desuetude, must give way before a bottom can be revealed. The end of Pburg (as locals call the town) or history or gray isn't really the end—there's something below. But to get to it the landscape's first got to be leveled, the kilns and the mill razed, the horizontal world abandoned.

"All memory resolves itself in gaze"—this is the second instance of oddly inflected syntax, and it's an interesting choice. Omitting the expected article creates a slight hitch in the reading, compelling attention, and compresses the word *gaze*, making it do the work of both noun and verb, mixing stasis and action, fusing space and time—the word is like a pivot, and the entire stanza turns on the phrase, bringing us to a fatal form of memory, an arrested, fixed memory that is now the only thing preventing total collapse, while at the same time offering *gaze*—gazing—as an action that might release the hold memory has on the horizontal. It's at this point in the poem that Hugo begins the move toward the salvational hopes of language, of poetry itself. He's down low, but not low enough yet to find his poem.

It seems to me a poet of Hugo's skill and knowledge can't possibly write this line without hearing the allusion to Orpheus. This is the heart of the poem, this is where it is. It happens quickly, reading like a toss-off, without a glance back, but I believe it's there. *Gaze* shows up in a similar passage in *The Merchant of Venice*, also about Orpheus, also about the poet's power to alter the quality of perception: "Their savage eyes turn'd to a modest gaze / By the sweet power of music: therefore the poet / Did feign that Orpheus . . ." Orpheus, whose lyre is now among the stars, is the figure of the poet and the poet's work. Nothing can withstand the charms of his music. Beasts are softened and lose their ferocity, stolid oaks move closer just to hear, rocks relax their hardness. Here it's probably worth mentioning—actually, it's vital to understanding—that Hugo's poem sits on top of the pastoral tradition, and certainly could be looked at as a failed bucolic. The poem seems to turn by shorthanding this rich, deep tradition. In Virgil's *Georgics* the story of Orpheus shows up strangely, in a treatise on bees, but has the passing character of a fertility myth. That the "green" in Hugo's poem is only "panoramic" at this point indicates how far from the regenerative power of all these vegetable myths Philipsburg is: there's no real sustenance in a panorama—or, as they say in Montana, you can't eat the scenery.

More important to Hugo's poem than the wide horizontal panorama is the idea of descent and depth implied in the Orpheus myth. Both are orders of vision, but they offer different things. Ovid gives Virgil's Orpheus a fuller treatment, the one people are familiar with, in which Eurydice, after her wedding to the poet, flees a seducer (Aristaeus, another poet and, not surprisingly, a beekeeper, who will subsequently suffer an apiary disaster) and is bitten by a snake and dies. Orpheus descends into the underworld to reclaim his bride. Along the way a fairy feeds him roasted ants, a flea's thigh, butterflies' brains, mites, a rainbow tart, all to be washed down with dewdrops and beer made of barleycorn—indicating, fabulously, the earthy depth of the poet's descent. In the underworld, as in the upper air, Orpheus sings his grief, and ghosts shed tears, Sisyphus sits on his rock to listen, Ixion's wheel stops its ceaseless revolving, Tantalus forgets his thirst, and the Furies, just this once, cry. But on his way back to the world, in an exact, cautionary lesson about one of the perils of artistic creation, Orpheus turns around, hoping to reassure himself, and loses his wife, who reaches out for a last embrace as she's drawn back toward death. Orpheus gives it another shot, but the underworld, whether in Chicago or Hades, is famously unforgiving, and second chances aren't available. In mourning, Orpheus seems to sicken with ennui, yet plays his lyre, wooing the inanimate world, wresting emotion from the trees and rocks, but eventually, forgoing women and loving boys, he's torn apart during a Bacchanalia by jealous Thracian maidens, and his severed head floats down the Hebrus, while his lyre, his poetry, is flung to the heavens.

If what distinguishes us from other members of the animal kingdom is speech, then literature—and poetry in particular, being the highest form of locution—is, to put it bluntly, the goal of our species.

—Joseph Brodsky

What's the deal with a poet who fills an entire stanza, fully a fourth of his poem, with questions? Part of it's just Hugo's standard battering style—where a single question might do, he pounds out a whole stanza— but again that style serves the subject. The heavy questions hammer away and demolish the mill that won't collapse. That Hugo's prosodic fist is big and blunt only makes it more suitable for the job. Each question—about the persistence of love, the pain of defeat, the scorn preventing desire—undercuts not only the binding failures of Philipsburg but also the poem's earlier assertions, turning us toward a kind of metacreation. The best way to come at this understanding is through the poem's back door. Desire in this stanza has an anachronistic, distinctly World War II flavor, with its blondes, booze, and jazz, and you sense Hugo's own swaggering, wounded self, his own haunting self-doubt, his own town, Seattle, needing to die inside. Suddenly it's no longer 1907 but 1947, and Hugo is back from the war, reaching down into a pain and hope that's personal. That's fine; it's his poem, after all. This slight historical warp is partly about Hugo's generous self-effacement, anyway; but it's also an oblique admission about the stake he has in the poem. In seeking hope for Philipsburg he begins to find hope for himself or, more accurately, for his poem. Here's the motivation, the stirring of desire, the first turn toward feeling necessary again. In much the same way that the myth of Orpheus elaborates a secondary tale about the act of creation, Hugo too gives us a poem about the making of poetry. The poem offers, somewhat covertly, an allegory of the poet's soul, caught in the terrifying process of creation. Why would anyone write a poem in this wrecked world? And really, how could they? Massive doubt, failed love, shitty thoughts, empty spirit, a dead history compelling a transfixed vision, these are devastations that might overwhelm and silence anyone; and silence, for a poet, is a prison. It's where the descent hits bottom, it's where the poet either faces or does not face all the risks of failed comprehension. It makes sense that Hugo would discover his reason for writing in a stanza so completely expressive of doubt. The critical difference between a poet and a regular citizen is that the poet seeks this realm; it's where he works, where his office is.

So, why questions? Everything in this stanza could be written using the indicative, flatly observed, or the ragging, hortatory imperative of a coach, urging us on. One answer might be that questions imply an auditor, the presence of another, and a stanza full of them suggests, by reaching out, some break in the isolation. Perhaps the questions are meant to prod an answer, but I kind of don't think so. Answers are as transient and foolish as we are, and poets generally aren't in the solution business. In fact, if you're a poet and you're going to pose questions, they'd better approach the unanswerable. Why? Is it that only questions without answers are worth asking? Is it that the muse needs courting and doesn't usually go with know-it-alls and wise guys? Is it that questions salt and preserve life, keeping the mystery fresh? Is it that any descent that hopes to claim our attention and hence a place in the record books is asterisked by answers, as if the poet, cheating, hadn't really touched bottom? In poetry, is the irritable reaching after answers (or certainties, as Keats put it) paradoxically just a type of doubt, a doubt about poetry itself? If rock bottom, if total bust for a poet is silence, then the questions must be unanswerable, without remedy, to provoke the central event, which is language. Answers are the end of speech, not the beginning, and if language is the main draw in poetry, silence is the occasion for it, the ground of renewal. Questions precede speech; they're language tensely coiled, expectant.

In the second stanza, the word *hatred* repeats, and now in the third stanza, it's *ring* we hear twice. It's an excellent, nearly echoic repetition, it rings, but it's also a curious choice; every connotation I can think of is almost purely positive. Clarity and resonance, calling, summons, proclamations, talk, producing sound, vibration, sonority—all meanings that counter the unanswerable questions, the testing of silence in the stanza. In my reading the aural quality of the word creates tension, making music of a different tenor than the literal subject. My ear hears something my eye doesn't quite see. The sound of *ring* rides on the surface of the stanza, separating from it somewhat. Whereas *hatred* draws us down into the core of the poem, *ring* begins to lift us out of it. Down deep in this stanza of questions, we hear a ringing, and it becomes possible to understand that Hugo's questions, their Orphic summons, aren't calling for an answer; they're calling for poetry.

How can one write poetry after Auschwitz?

—critic Theodor Adorno

And how can one eat lunch?

—poet Mark Strand

"Say no to yourself"—if only Orpheus had, if only he'd refused the unsure, doubting, rearward glance, he'd have spent that first night back in the upper air abed with his bride. Instead, his hesitation breaks the lyric charm and condemns Eurydice to death. The temptation, in art as well as life, is to fall back on old forms, to attempt an impossible repetition, giving yourself over to the sort of redundancy that has always been the defining feature of the underworld, where time is either a torment or means nothing because the iterations are endless and unvarying. Hell is crowded not because sinners are commonplace but because in-completion is the norm. Orpheus, descending, charms the underworld, he moves it toward an uncharacter-istic stillness and rest, but in ascending, it's as if his hesitation, his glance back, were suddenly an affliction no different from the thirst of Tantalus or the labor of Sisyphus. Because he looks back, losing his bride, his work remains unfinished, forever, and the sorrow he can't overcome results in a sort of hypnotic hindsight. "Saying no" is necessary; it too is part of the process of creation. After saying yes to the descent, saying no is how the poet emerges. Perhaps another way of articulating this is to say that a new yes must be found, the courage of the descent sustained until it's completed. In a poem the future, or the next couple dozen words anyway (which to a poet is the same thing), is the poem. The need is finally aesthetic. Hugo's final stanza is a return to speech, referenced phrasally throughout: "say no, he says, you tell, you're talking." But the return is premised on not looking back, on avoiding the gaze that tempts and paralyzes memory. Unlike Orpheus, the poet here says no and, in true Western fashion, gets the girl, who happens to be slender, with red hair that lights the wall.

It's not the sort of refusal it might first seem—seemed to me, anyway. It's not a turning away, an opting out of history, an easy escape. To push the metapoetic reading, the car, that absent term from the first stanza, still runs, as does life, but on this newly accessed level of understanding, I think it's also fair to say that another of the missing, implied terms is poetry itself. Poetry is the vehicle that broke down and brought Hugo here, to the degrees of gray, but it still runs, and the proof is the poem itself. The poem is what the poet brings back, that's his fortune, his Eurydice. You can imagine these words lost among broken symbols, dragged off by history, sunk in silence, but that isn't what we have. Not answers but aesthetic pressure completes the poem. In the end, it doesn't matter that the light reveals a wall that will likely never come down entirely. "Let us not look for the door, and the way out," Camus wrote, "anywhere but in the wall against which we are living." The irony, the slight undertone pulling at Hugo's last word, tempers the jubilance with a doubt, but suggests that in this prison, shared by all, life is still possible. Fortuna is sometimes depicted wearing a blindfold, and the light in the final line really refers to the act of seeing. It's about optics more than opportunity. The poem is the light.

Tonight was the Fourth of July, and another order of light was at work, flaring in the sky over these same streets. It was a disorganized display, mostly people in their backyards firing rockets that shot up, burst, fell, and faded, somewhat emptily, in this vast valley. I walked to town because I needed to double-check the streets of Philipsburg and square what I saw with the falling man's incomprehensible descent. I wanted to think just a little more about Hugo and the place of poetry in the face of terrible things. I stopped by a green house above Main Street where, all last winter, dogs fought over the carcasses of several deer. I remembered the rib cages marbled red and white with blood and fat and the ruts of stained red snow where the warring dogs dragged the bones, but when I passed by tonight I saw the house had been boarded up, the tenant gone in a going that doesn't really hold much mystery, not here in Philipsburg. What's another absence, another vacancy? But if this uncelebrated loss means nothing I can't see how the falling man's descent acquires true significance either. Consensus isn't an answer. Mining towns in Montana or Kentucky that have collapsed over the course of a century have suffered a descent as murderous as a moment in New York, but history has hidden those deaths and numbed the witnesses and litanized their loss under the rubric of progress. In the case of Philipsburg, only a poet spoke out, from his own isolation, to say something about the devastating pain.

Still, ruin, nearly as much as a good poem, is strangely enduring. The hills behind Philipsburg are full of things that have failed to remain upright. Poets might not save, but the clichés surrounding September 11 didn't stop anything either, and in this sense the score, in the game of language, is decisively on the side of poetry. If forced to choose between failures, poetry is probably the better one. The difference between the truth and a cliché is the difference between what we really know and what we've all heard about.

That diversity is good is a slogan we've all heard, but it has expressive limits—it's not OK to fly jets into office buildings—and so what does it really mean? For me, borrowing from Isaiah Berlin, another writer intimately aware of history, diversity (or plurality) is an answer to the central twentieth-century historical problem of radical subjectivity. Accumulating enough subjectivities—setting them against each other—is as close as we're going to come to objectivity, and this is why agreement is problematic: What's the point of being right if it's only safety in numbers? The history of being right and how wrong it's turned out to be is a long one. By this measure the terrorists were wrong—such empty holiness is almost too much to bear in mind—but when being right provides comfort, when the sensation of it is pleasant, when it allays anxiety or lends security, then it seems to be doing the job of ignorance. If we're right, then the nature and quality and burden of being right is our issue. Now it seems time to argue for the tragic or the absurd, for anything that tempers and draws limits. Sometimes contradiction can't be resolved away and then it becomes the new reality and there's no way out. The falling man is enormously sad and insignificant; he is everything as well as nothing. The only way into his descent is through our solitude. Patriotism's just a rag we fly over the silence.

In *Mimesis*, Erich Auerbach's book on the represen-
tation of reality in Western literature, he talks of the
shift from antiquity to a New Testament style of realism. "To be sure," he writes, "we must not forget that
the transformation is here one whose course progresses
to somewhere outside of history, to the end of time or
to the coincidence of all times, in other words upward,
and does not . . . remain on the horizontal plane of
historical events." I wonder, was our understanding of
September 11 little more than a Christian homily, an
escape from history, a romance secularizing the divine
or lifting the legend out of the ruin—is that where it
all went? All through the writing of this I thought of
Shelley, who at eighteen sent copies of a pamphlet on
atheism to every professor at Oxford. He believed a
university dedicated to open discussion and the free
exchange of ideas would be interested. He was kicked
out. Next he went to Ireland, planning to begin a major rehabilitation of all mankind by organizing the Irish
into a "society of peace and love," perhaps a doomed
enterprise. Next he was off to Wales, again with a pamphlet, this one called "A Declaration of Rights." He enclosed copies in dark-green bottles that he sealed with
wax and cast into the ocean; other copies he floated
aloft, to be blown inland on balloons. Is it reasonable
to think Shelley was eternally part of mankind in his

solitary foolish hope at sea's edge? That his solitude was the mark of a deeper, broader inclusion? Or is this just poetic fancy? Watching the fireworks made me wonder. In general I don't care for activities—fireworks or football or movies—where large groups of people gather and look at the same thing. This is probably just a queerness of temperament. Maybe I don't like crowds. Regardless, the fireworks rose up, pulsing in our local cosmos. On the way home I stopped to watch the show with some kids who were heaped under blankets while the parents handled the pyrotechnics. Each explosion eclipsed the sky with dazzling colors and froze the onlooking, upturned faces like a strobe. All the kids kept pointing up, the way astonished kids will, as if I might not know where to look.

From The Spirit of History

When gold paint flakes from the arms of sculptures,
When the letter falls out of the book of laws,
Then consciousness is naked as an eye.

When the pages of books fall in fiery scraps
Onto smashed leaves and twisted metal,
The tree of good and evil is stripped bare.

Charles D'Ambrosio

When a wing made of canvas is extinguished
In a potato patch, when steel disintegrates,
Nothing is left but straw and cow dung.

———————

I rolled a cigarette and licked the paper.
Then a match in the little house of my hand.
And why not a tinderbox with a flint?
The wind was blowing. I sat on the road at noon,
Thinking and thinking. Beside me, potatoes.

—Czesław Miłosz

The following essays appeared first in *The Stranger*: "Seattle, 1974"; "Loitering" (as "The Crime That Never Was"); "Whaling Out West" (as "Whaling"); and "Casting Stones" as ("Mary Kay Letourneau"). "Seattle, 1974" also appeared in *The Eleventh Draft: Craft and the Writing Life from the Iowa Writers' Workshop*, ed. Frank Conroy. "Any Resemblance to Anyone Living" and "Misreading" (as "True Believer") appeared first in *Tin House*. "Documents" and "Catching Out" (as "Train in Vain") appeared originally in *The New Yorker*. "American Newness" (as "Modular Homes"), "Winning" (as "Brick Wall"), "One More Paradise" as ("Biosquat"), and "Orphans" were first published in *Nest: A Quarterly of Interiors*. "Brick Wall" also appeared in *Harper's*. "Doo-Wop Down the Road" was published in Camela Raymond's much-loved broadsheet, *The Organ*. "Salinger and Sobs" appeared first in *With Love and Squalor*, eds. Kip Kotzen and Thomas Beller, and was subsequently collected in *The Story About the Story: Great Writers Explore Great Literature*, ed. J. C. Hallman. A portion of "This Is Living" was published in *Money Changes Everything*, eds. Jenny Offill and Elissa Schappell. "Degrees of Gray in Philipsburg" first saw print in an anthology called *The Clear Cut Future*.

Copyright Notes & Permissions

Acknowledgements

I'd like to begin by paying overdue tribute to one of the most naturally curious men I've ever known, Rich Jensen, for bringing the bold and visionary ambitions of Clear Cut Press to life. Like most writers, I've benefited from wise and tolerant editors everywhere, but because I have a weak spot for Seattle's great alt-weekly, *The Stranger*, I can't resist singling out some key figures by name: Matthew Stadler, Emily White, Sean Nelson, Charles Mudede, and Christopher Frizzelle. I'm not easy, and no one knows that better than Mary Evans and Jordan Pavlin, to whom I owe so much. For her quiet behind-the-scenes advice and guidance over many years, thank you, Jody. For offering an open hand, thank you, Lee Montgomery. For her friendship, fierce intelligence, and keen eye, thank you, Sarah Fay. For their generous and always timely support I'd like to thank the Whiting Foundation, the American Academy of Arts and Letters, the Lannan Foundation, and United States Artists. And finally to the whole Tin House family, who make so many things happen, I want to thank each and every one of you—Diane Chonette, Lance Cleland, Masie Cochran, Matthew Dickman, Emma Komlos-Hrobsky, Cheston Knapp, Holly MacArthur, Nanci McCloskey, Tony Perez, Thomas Ross, Elissa Schappell, Rob Spillman, Meg Storey, Jakob Vala, Michelle Wildgen, and, of course, Win McCormack—for making this book happen.

CHARLES D'AMBROSIO is the author of two collections of short stories, *The Point* and *The Dead Fish Museum*, which was a finalist for the PEN/Faulkner Award, and the essay collection *Orphans*. He's been the recipient of a Whiting Writer's Award and a Lannan Fellowship, among other honors. His work has appeared frequently in *The New Yorker*, as well as in *Tin House*, *The Paris Review*, *Zoetrope All-Story*, and *A Public Space*. He teaches fiction at the Iowa Writers' Workshop.